JUST GLAD THINGS

By
Edgar A. Guest

DETROIT ------ MICHIGAN
1911

IT would not do to say to you
    That in this book of mine
Is reading matter strictly new,
    Nor is that my design.
Far better have these songs been sung
    Than ever I could trill them;
The ancients, when the world was young,
    (See Homer) used to kill them.

There's nothing new upon this earth,
    In thought or song or story;
The good old-timers had their mirth,
    And dealt in allegory.
Each new song is but ancient dope,
    And none but fools deny it;
This little book is --- still I hope
    In spite of that you'll buy it.

TO THE GLAD MEN AND WOMEN Who Make This World Beautiful;

TO ALL Who Make the Best of the Worst and the Most of the Best;

TO THE MANY Who Suffer Patiently and Without Complaint;

TO EVERY Cheerful Heart and Smiling Face; And Especially

TO ALL Who Are Glad To Buy This Book, This Humble Collection of "Just Glad Things" Is Affectionately Dedicated. E. A. G.

Contents

Just
Glad
Things

THINK HAPPY THOUGHTS

THINK happy thoughts!
Think sunshine all the day;
Refuse to let the trifling worries stay,
Crowd them with thoughts of laughter from your mind.
Think of the good, forget the bad you find,
Think of the sun behind the clouds; the blue
And not the gray skies that you view.
Think of the kindness not the meanness shown,
The true friends not the false ones you have known;
The joy and not the hatred of the strife,
The sweetness not the bitterness of life.
Think happy thoughts!

Think happy thoughts!
Think always of the best,
Think of the ones you love, not those that you detest;
Think of your victories and not your failures here,
The smile that pleased and not the hurtful sneer,
The kindly word and not the harsh word spoken,
The promise kept and not the promise broken;
The good that you have known and not the bad,
The happy days that were and not the sad;
Think of the rose and not the withered flower,
The beauty of the rainbow, not the shower.
Think happy thoughts!

Think happy thoughts!
This is true happiness!
That life is sad that feeds on its distress;
That mind is gloomy that subsists on gloom,
And is as dismal as a curtained room,

Where daily comes the sunshine, but to find
It cannot enter through the close-drawn blind.
Fling up the curtains of your mind today
And let the morning sunshine in to play;
Dwell on the joys and not the sorrows here,
Master your thoughts and you have mastered fear.
Think happy thoughts!

THE GLORY OF AGE

"WHAT is the glory of age?" I said,
"A hoard of gold and a few dear friends?
When you 've reached the day that you look ahead
And see the place where your journey ends,
When Time has robbed you of youthful might ---
What is the secret of your delight?"

And an old man smiled as he answered me:
"The glory of age is n't gold or friends,
When we 've reached the valley of Soon-To-Be
And note the place where our journey ends;
The glory of age, be it understood,
Is a boy out there who is making good.

"The greatest joy that can come to man
When his sight is dim and his hair is gray;
The greatest glory that God can plan
To cheer the lives of the old today,
When they no more share in the battle yell,
Is a boy out there who is doing well."

THE KILLING PACE

WE 'RE hiking along at a two-forty pace
We 're making life seem like a man-killing race,
With our nerves all on edge and our jaws firmly set
We go rushing along; with our brows lined with sweat
And our cheeks pale and drawn every minute we dash,
And the goal that we 're after is merely more cash.

We 're out for the money, the greenbacks and gold,
We 're all scared to death we 'll be poor when we're old;
We want the mazuma, and want it right now,
And we spend all our time at the desk and the plow,
We 're working like navvies, refusing to see
The gold of the sun and the green of the tree.

We 've got in a rut that the dollar sign dug,
And we 're plainly obessed by the millionaire bug;
We 've loaded our backs till they bend with the strain
And we lug and we tug at our burdens in vain;
With never a minute for laughter and fun,
Or the green of the tree and the gold of the sun.

A few of us land in the millionaire class,
But only to find that our gold is all brass;
That the money we 've got we would gladly give back
For a stomach and liver that were n't out of whack;
For legs that were supple and eyes that could see
The gold of the sun and the green of the tree.

The trouble with us is we 're working too hard,
We ought to get out with the kids in the yard,
We ought to let slip a few dollars to play
With the friends that we love, and we ought to be gay;
The pace is too fast for our nerves and our health,
We should laugh more and cut out this chase after wealth.

THE WAY OF THE WORLD

IT 'S ALL in the way that you look at the world,
It 's all in the way that you do things,
With laughter or sorrow your lips may be curled,
But it 's all in the way that you view things.
Yes, it 's all in the way that you journey along
That makes life a plague or a pleasure,
The mind is the fountain of wailing or song
And a man is the judge of the measure.

It 's all in the way that you look at your woe
And not in the woe that is sent you;
You may bear it with courage and smile as you go,
Or frown and let it discontent you.
For care is a creature that 's born of the mind,
And gloom is a cloud we can scatter,
The thorn of the rose if we seek we can find,
But the thorn of the rose does n't matter.

We can make our own sunshine and make our own mirth,
We can add to our trouble by moping;
We can make a grim graveyard of this glad old earth
By giving up loving and hoping.
For it 's all in the way that we look at the world,
Yes, it 's all in the way that we view things,
With sorrow or laughter our lips may be curled
For it 's all in the way that we do things.

¶ The man who minds his own business may not always succeed but he has everything in his favor.

WHAT TO DO

IF I had wealth and I had health,
And I 'd a roof above me,
If I 'd a wife to cheer my life,
But not one child to love me,
No rosy-lipped young laughing miss,
No bright-eyed, roguish laddie,
I 'd search the town, both up and down,
Till one should call me daddie.

I would not have a roof that ne'er
Knew sound of childish chatter,
Nor keep a floor, untottered o'er
By little feet that patter.
Nor would I hang upon my walls
Great pictures, just to show them,
Unless a tot had left a lot
Of finger-marks below them.

I would not like to settle down
Within my old armchair,
And take my ease, with empty knees ---
I want a youngster there.
Likewise with everything I have,
How incomplete 't would be,
Unless I had a girl or lad
To share it all with me.

And so I say if I had wealth,
And had a roof above me.
If I 'd a wife to cheer my life,
But had no child to love me,
Then I would search both up and down,
To beg or buy or borrow,
A child to be a part of me ---
I 'd have one here tomorrow.

THE BANK CLERK

I'D LIKE to be a bank clerk, and sit inside a cage,
I 'd like to take and hoard away the toiler's weekly wage;
I 'd like to sit behind a drawer with gold and greenbacks lined,
I 'd like to read the writing on the checks rich men have signed,
It must be nice to shut up shop at 3 and cease to fret,
And then I wish that I could have the holidays they get.

I 'd like to be a bank clerk, with a pen behind my ear,
To go to work at 9 and know that quitting time 's so near:
To occupy a cage in which no office bores can sit,
With nothing else to do but take in cash and care for it.
I 'd like to be a bank clerk; that I 'm not is my regret;
Just think of all the holidays the weary bank clerks get.

I love the name of Lincoln and the name of Washington,
I like to think about the way George made the British run;
I 'd like to take a day off, too, to honor him, I say,
And I would also like to rest on Decoration Day;
I love this land of freedom, and I like to sing her praise,
But I wish I were a bank clerk to enjoy her holidays.

¶ If a hen did her cackling before she laid an egg, how like a lot of men she would be.

THE DREAM DAYS

I LIKE the dream days best of all,
The hollyhocks against the wall;
The rambler roses blushing red,
The blue skies bending overhead,
With just enough of summer breeze
To whisper in the leafy trees;
When lazily the plow boys plod,
And lazily the blossoms nod,
And everything about me seems
Wrapt up somehow in pleasant dreams.

I like to lie full length and flat,
And shade my eyes with my old hat;
Building out yonder in the skies
Air castles grand, whose towers rise
Higher than summer swallows fly,
The castles of sweet by and by;
Forgetting care and shirking toil,
Forgetting lust for fame and spoil,
Just dreaming dreams that won't come true,
But living as the flowers do.

I like the dream days best, for then
The world 's in tune with lazy men;
The very flowers droop and sway
In such a restful, lazy way
As though they, too, would like to be
Stretched out beneath this tree with me;
And fleecy, snow white clouds float by
As though no part of earth or sky.
And far off seem the busy marts
Where gather shrewd and sordid hearts,
Just roses, hollyhocks and I,
Dreaming while Father Time goes by.

SOMEBODY SPOKE A CHEERING WORD

SOMEBODY spoke a cheering word,
Somebody praised his labor,
And something deep in his soul was stirred,
That night he smiled at his neighbor.
He kissed his wife with a hearty smack,
He rode the children upon his back
And he sang a tuneful ditty,
"Ho, ho," he cried to his patient wife,
"I vow that never in all my life
Have I seen you look so pretty."

Then into her eyes the love light crept,
A smile on her face appeared,
She hummed a song as the room she swept,
And the children tugged his beard.
He told them stories of fairies good,
Of pixies out in the distant wood,
And the sailors on the sea;
And there was a family made gay
Just because somebody chanced to say
One little word cheerfully.

And nobody knows how far it went,
And nobody here can say
When the morning came and he bravely went
To his labors for the day,
How much of the courage he showed was due
To the smile and the cheering word or two;
But this we know, anyhow,
That he climbed the ladder to wealth and fame,
And a cheering word may do the same
For somebody else right now.

GETTING HER A VALENTINE

"GIVE me the prettiest valentine
You 've got in the shop," said he,
"One with the tenderest sort o' line,
In type that her eyes can see.
One that she won't need her specs to read,
'I love you my darling,' is all I need.

"A line o' love from an old bald head,
An' a throb from a battered heart;
An old skeezicks, with a feeble tread,
A lover, no longer smart.
An' she ain't as young as she used t' be,
But she looks for her valentine still from me.

"I wish they made old folks' valentines,
With gray heads close together;
An' printed 'em, too, with loving lines
About fair and stormy weather,
An' showed the old man an' his gray-haired wife
Walking arm in arm on the edge of life.

"We 've traveled the road from youth to age,
Without missin' a single kiss;
In our book o' life every written page
Has something o' joy and bliss,
An' though it ain't long till we go above,
We 're nearing the end with a load o' love.

"So give me your prettiest valentine,
An' I 'll send it along today
To that wonderful old sweetheart o' mine,
Whose tresses are thin and gray.
But I wish they made valentines," said he,
"For seventy-year lovers like ma an' me."

THE CHOIR AT PIXLEY

THE choir we had in Pixley was n't much for looks an' styles,
But today if I could hear it I would walk a hundred miles;
There warn't a singer in it that could boast she 'd crossed the seas
To study with the masters and to learn to make high C's;
There warn't no variations, warn't no frills that folks think grand;
Warn't no singin' operatic that no one can understand;
But jus' plain gospel singin' like the music of the birds,
An' the congregation did n't have to strain to catch the words.

There were jus' four people in it --- Mrs. Tompkins, Mrs. Botts,
Arthur Tweedle was the tenor, an' the basso Jeptha Watts.
Oh, 't would do you good to hear 'em singin' low "Abide With Me,"
An' "Jerusalem the Golden" an' "The City by the Sea."
There was nothin' high-falutin' 'bout the songs they used t' sing,
Jus' sweet, humble hymns of praises to the Master an' the King;
Jus' sweet, simple strains of music, but my soul they always stirred,
An' I liked it better, mebbe, coz I understood each word.

An' I mind the day in Pixley when a city woman came
To our little church to visit, an' I mind her burnin' shame,
When she sneered about the singin' an' she scoffed about the choir,
An' I mind the way she snickered an' the way she roused my ire,
An' how I up and told her that the music she thought grand
Was the music that she paid for an' she could n't understand;
An' I said the choir ain't singin' now for you, an' never would,
But it 's singin' for the Master an' I guess He 'd call it good.

The little church in Pixley ain't a little church no more,
It 's took in wealthy people an' its steeples skyward soar;
It 's got a marble altar an' it 's got a tony choir
Of singers trained in Europe an' a-singin' now for hire.
They 're runnin' now to solos an' they advertise the fact
That So and So is goin' t' sing, a large crowd to attract;
But I can't say I like it, why it is n't half so good
As the little choir that used t' sing the songs we understood.

BUCKLE IN

JUST about the time the clouds are blackest
Let your thoughts go roving to the sun,
Just about the time your job is hardest
Think how glad you 'll be when it is done.
Buckle to the task that you are facing,
Work away and pretty soon you 'll find
All the little difficulties vanished,
All the little worries far behind.

'T is n't any use to sit and whimper,
Does n't help a bit to sit and sigh,
Lose yourself in working out the problem,
If it 's hard just buckle in and try.
Do n't waste time in thinking what may happen,
Plug along and do the best you can,
That 's the way to show the stuff you 're made of,
That 's the way to prove yourself a man.

¶ Getting rich is only the first hurdle in the race to success. Making good with the money after we get it is the big barrier that most of us stumble at.

A wise man forgets half his grievances and pays no attention to the other half.

When everything is said and done,
The wife who nags
Is better company, I find,
Than is the man who brags.

Half the smiles that we see are n't really genuine, but the fact that they are forced makes them all the more worthy.

A PLACE AT THE TOP

THERE 'S a place for you at the top, my boy,
Are you willing to try to get it?
It 's true that trouble will try to stop
Your efforts, but will you let it?
The road is long and the path is rough,
Designed for men of the proper stuff,
And you can't get by with a common bluff,
For the way is barred to bluffers.
And ever and ever the weak drop out,
But the strong keep going with courage stout;
They may taste defeat, but never rout,
But it 's worth all a fighter suffers.

Up there at the top there 's a place for you,
You may earn it or let it go;
And the world won't care which of these you do,
It 's up to yourself to show
Whether you can battle with fate and wrong,
And take hard luck when it comes along
With a nervy grin or a bit of song
Or stop with the quitters tamely.
There 's room at the top; you can get there, too,
If you 're ready to fight your own way through.
The odds are heavy, I know, but you
Can win, if you 'll face them gamely.

¶ The difference between true love and the near-stuff is that true love goes out and gets a job when she finds that she has taken her husband for worse, while the near-article hustles to the divorce court.

THE WAY TO MAKE FRIENDS

THE way to make friends is as easy
As breathing the fresh morning air;
It is n't an art to be studied
Alone by the men who can spare
The time from their every day labors,
To ponder on classical lore,
It never is taught in a college
And it is n't a trick or a chore.

The way to make friends is to be one,
To smile at the stranger you meet,
To think cheerful thoughts and to speak them
Aloud to the people you greet.
To hold your hand out to a brother,
And cheerfully say: "Howdy-do,"
In a way that he 'll know that you mean it,
That 's all that 's expected of you.

Be honest in all of your dealings,
Be true to your word and your home,
And you will make friends, never doubt it,
Wherever you happen to roam.
Condemn not the brother who falters,
Nor fawn on the rich and the great.
Speak kindly to all who approach you,
And give up all whining at fate.

¶ Trying to get rich quick is what keeps a lot of men poor.

THE COST OF PRAISE

THIS morning came a man to me, his smile was wonderful to see,
He shook my hand and doffed his hat then promptly took a chair;
Said he, "I read your stuff each day, and I have just dropped in to say
You have a line of humor that delightful is and rare.
My dear wife reads it through and through, my aunts and uncles like it, too,
The little children cry for it when they get out of bed,
Your column 's full of common sense, your childhood verses are immense,
The equal of them, I am sure I 've never, never read.

"Now, you 're a man of great renown, your name is known in every town
From Boston unto 'Frisco, from Atlanta to Duluth;
I 've met some of our famous men, I wish to grasp your hand again;
Do n't think I flatter you, O no, I 'm telling you the truth."
I let him once more take my hand, the while I felt my chest expand,
My head began to bulge until I could n't wear my hat;
"Ah me," I sighed, "through all my days, I 've never heard such words of praise,
I wish I knew a hundred men who 'd talk to me like that."

"And now," said he, "ere I forget, I want to show a Balzac set
That Jolliers have printed just especially for you;

There are but twenty-six of these, observe this small
prospectus, please,
This is the finest work that any publisher can do.
For you we make this sacrifice, just sixty dollars is
the price,
Five dollars down and three a month---you will not
miss the 'mon.'"
I signed away my salary. Henceforth, when men
come praising me
I'm going to grab my hat and coat and exit on the
run.

LITERARY MOTHER

HUSH, little ones don't make a noise
Pick up your dolls and pick up your toys,
Pick up your Teddy Bear, Johnny, now see
How quiet a youngster tonight you can be;
Daddy will wash up the dishes, while you
Quietly sit there to wait till he's through;
Softly about we must tread on tip-toe,
Mother is writing a paper on Poe.

What is that noise? It's the scratch of her pen,
Mother has locked herself into my den,
Gone there to study, to ponder and write,
And we must give up all our laughter tonight.
Hush, there! Don't giggle. Be still while I sweep
And see just how quiet you children can keep.
Hey, there, you Johnny, don't romp about so,
Mother is writing a paper on Poe.

Come, now, you two-year-old, father will try
To put on your nightie and rock you bye, bye;

And, Johnny, you sit on the floor and take off
Your shoes and your stockings. Look out, do n't you
cough.
Poor kids, you 've no mother tonight to undress you,
To sing you to sleep and to love and caress you,
Just an awkward old daddy, whose fingers are slow,
But then mother 's writing a paper on Poe.

Oh, literature is a wonderful thing,
Of joy and delight a perennial Spring.
But gee! it is tough on the kids and their dad,
Who think that the evening 's the time to be glad;
And sometimes I think that the art is pernicious,
And often I wish mother was n't ambitious,
Tonight as I sit here and rock to and fro,
All alone, I am cursing that paper on Poe.

¶ Some women declare that it is better to be a chaperone than never to see a good show at all.

A pretty girl does n't have to know how to cook, but she 's got a tremendous advantage if she does.

Life insurance makes any widow attractive.

There was a young fellow named Fred,
In an aeroplane flew over head;
His baragraph showed
He had been where it snowed,
But his epitaph shows that he 's dead.

All the world 's a stage, but few of us are property men.

Never judge the value of a man's speech by the length of it.

OTHER'S SUCCESSES

CAN you go to another who wins in the fight
And give him a hand-shake that 's true?
Do you find yourself feeling a sense of delight
In the good work another may do?
Or deep in your heart are there envy and hate,
When you see someone getting ahead?
Do you sneer at his luck and rail at your fate?
If you do all your courage has fled.

If you have n't learned to rejoice in the deed
Of your brothers and give them a cheer,
You have n't discovered the pathways that lead
To genuine happiness here.
If you cannot say to a brother, " I 'm glad
You have conquered," and give him your hand,
Your life must be gloomy and woefully sad,
You 're building your mansion on sand.

Did you secretly gloat when another had failed,
Did you sneer at the efforts he made?
Did it inwardly please you to see him assailed,
Did you chuckle to see him outplayed?
If this is the part you have chosen to play,
If you are as selfish as this,
Though he falls in the thick and the heat of the fray,
Your failure is greater than his.

¶ A wise man lets a woman have the last word early in the argument.

GOOD FRIDAY

O, SAD and solemn holy day,
O, bitterest of bitter hours!
Behold He staggers on His way
Beneath the cross that saps His powers.
O, see, they goad Him with their thongs,
And mock Him as He falters there,
For us, for us He bears these wrongs
And goes the crown of thorns to wear.

No word of bitterness He speaks,
No look of hatred mars His face,
The scoffers spit upon His cheeks
And taunt Him in the market place;
And now upon the cross He 's nailed,
"I thirst," He mutters, that is all;
But still He is to be assailed,
His lips must taste the cup of gall.

Once more His lips are seen to move,
O, holy sentence uttered there!
What more His love could better prove
Than these few words borne on the air:
"Father, forgive them," thus He prayed,
And doubt you that His love was true?
Still patient, gentle, unafraid,
"Forgive, they know not what they do."

For us the crown of thorns He wore
With patience man has never known;
For us the cruel cross He bore
With meekness man has never shown.
For us He lived, for us He died,
O, sad and solemn holy day,
Renouncing self and earthly pride
That we might know the better way.

MAGAZINE GIRLS

ALL women are lovely and radiantly fair
In the magazine pages today,
They all have a mop of luxuriant hair,
In the magazine pages today.
There 's not one with freckles or nose gone askew,
Or teeth that protrude, as some real girls' do,
There is n't a blemish on girls that we view
In the magazine pages today.

There 's not one too pudgy or not one too thin,
In the magazine pages today;
Nor one who 's just losing her tortoise shell pin,
In the magazine pages today.
'Twixt shirtwaist and belt there is never a gap,
Or a tear in the silk that is lining her wrap,
And her gloves never lack a pearl button or snap,
In the magazine pages today.

She does n't wear pink when she ought to wear blue,
In the magazine pages today;
And she is n't run down at the heel of her shoe,
In the magazine pages today.
You never can see when she has n't a hat,
How much is real hair and how much of it 's rat,
It 's only in real life that we see things like that,
Not in magazine pages today.

¶ Women rejoice over a new leaf on the rubber plant. Men grieve because every new leaf makes it only that much heavier to lug in and out when it rains.

THE REWARDS OF INDUSTRY

A FRIEND of mine said yesterday: "There goes a man across the way
Who paid ten thousand dollars for a home a week ago;
He owns an automobile now, a saddle horse and keeps a cow,
And smokes cigars at fifty cents a throw.
He is a lucky chap, indeed! He got up something that we need,
The way he 's making money is a shame;
It 's not five years ago, I swear, he only had one suit to wear
And did n't have a dollar to his name.

" There goes a man immensely rich, who was a digger in the ditch
Ten years ago, but fortune came his way;
I cannot now recall to mind just what it is that he designed,
But he got wealth and glory in a day.
How fortunate some fellows are! They 're born beneath a lucky star ---
I knew him when he did n't have a cent;
And now he owns his house and lot --- Too bad, that 's something I 've forgot,
I don 't know now just what he did invent."

I said: " Some fellows strike it rich, but somehow, I 've a notion, which
Is that you never saw a lucky shirk;
I never knew a lazy moke that was n't nearly always broke ---

The men who get the money have to work.
I do not view with discontent, nor call them lucky who invent
The things that quickly bring great fortunes in;
The poor men of five years ago, who now possess a 'wad of dough'
But prove to me that industry can win."

¶ Good company always knows when to go home.

THE INFLUENCE OF WOMAN

WHAT would be the use of singing songs
If there was no little woman near to hear them?
What would be the use of righting wrongs
If a little woman did n't cease to fear them?
What would be the use of getting rich,
Oh, what would be the use of winning fame,
If the conquest was n't really something which
Brought glory to a little woman's name?

What would be the use of all the striving,
The turmoil and the heartache and the sighs?
Who would bear the goad of ceaseless driving
If it was n't for the lovelight in her eyes?
If it was n't for a woman's tender glances,
Who waits at home with welcome fond and true,
If we ever ceased to live our sweet romances,
What would be the use of all we do?

THE TOWN OF NOTHING-TO-DO

THEY say somewhere in the distance fair,
Is the town of Nothing-to-Do,
Where the sun, they say, shines every day
And the skies are always blue;
Where no one tries for a silver prize
And no one strives for gold,
There, every race has taken place,
And every tale been told.

The blacksmith sings as his anvil rings
Of the town of Nothing-to-Do,
And vows in his song, though the road is long
When with anvil and forge he 's through
He will wander far, where the glad folks are,
And will rest in that happy town;
He dreams of the day when he 'll put for aye
His apron and hammer down.

O, it matters not what the toiler's lot,
Be he preacher or soldier brave,
Though he delve a ditch, be he great or rich,
Be judge or a statesman grave,
He dreams always of the future days
When he 'll go to Nothing-to-Do,
When he 's faced life's test, and his hands will rest
And his time of toil is through.

But Nothing-to-Do, folks tell me, who
Have journeyed the hills and found it,
Is a hollow fake and a big mistake,
For the streams of care surround it.
And the people there, they all declare,
Are gloomy and sad and sighing,
And they yearn for strife, for the joy of life
Is something to do worth trying.

LIFE AND HEREAFTER

NOT over there do I await
Reward for patience here below,
Not over there at Heaven's gate
Is all the joy that I shall know;
Not for the joys to be am I
Seeking the better, truer way,
All pleasure 's not beyond the sky,
For I have my reward each day.

I hope for Heaven and all it means,
And hope to hear the Master tell,
When I have quit these earthly scenes,
That I have truly toiled and well;
But not alone for that I strive
To keep my soul unspotted here,
Honor has joys for all alive
That are as infinitely dear.

What can the great hereafter give
More precious than my children's love,
When I, on earth, shall cease to live,
And go to join the realms above?
Were there no future, then I say
I still should strive to faithful be,
That they would run at close of day
With loving arms to welcome me.

A baby's kiss, a faithful wife,
And friends who trust, are not these all
Rewards that honor earns in life,
Although your hoard of gold be small?
And though there were no future, would
You still not journey on your way
Striving, as ever, to be good
Just for the joys you know today?

And so I say, not "over there,"
Do I sit sighing, "I shall know
The perfect bliss, with ne'er a care"---
The perfect bliss is here below.
Nor do I dream of joys to be,
And wail the cares that now are mine,
Earth's glories now appeal to me,
And this life is almost divine.

¶ Some men mistake conceit for dignity.

A VALENTINE

YOUR cheeks are pinker than the rose,
Your eyes are bluer than the skies;
Than you no fairer blossom grows,
In you all earthly sweetness lies.
Without you life were drear to me,
I dream of you the night long through;
Oh, sweetheart! hear my humble plea:
Please let me hook your waists for you.

Your voice is sweet as song of birds,
Your eyes would shame the stars above;
There is no power in written words
To truly tell you how I love.
When I 'm with you I 'm trouble free,
But absent, desolate and blue,
Darling, I pray you 'll hear my plea:
Please let me hook your waists for you.

AN UNCLE

BEIN' uncle to the kids,
Laughin' lips an' drowsy lids
Grimy hands an' tattered clothes,
Cheeks as red as any rose;
Willie Browns an' Jimmy Whites,
Sarah Smiths an' Mabel Brights;
One an' all I 'm glad t' see,
Love t' hear 'em "uncle" me.

Want no child t' "mister" me,
Do n't want no formality,
When a youngster 's playin' round,
Uncle has a sweeter sound;
Seems there 's somethin' in the name,
Takes your heart an' grips the same
In a way that makes you feel
Love is somethin' that is real.

Been their uncle now for years,
I have brushed away the tears
Of the little tots when they
Hurt themselves while at their play;
Nursed stone bruises. When they fell
Kissed the lumps t' make 'em well;
Seen 'em grow t' handsome men,
Uncle to their children then.

Ruther be an uncle than
Any other famous man;
Ruther have the children come
Blowin' horn an' beatin' drum
After me, when I go by,
Laughin' like a summer sky,
Than be great, an' miss the joys
Of the little girls an' boys.

THE BRIGHT SIDE

KINDER like to see the bright side,
See the gay and dancing light side,
See the good and decent right side
Of the worst that happens me;
For the gloomy and the glum side,
And the " worst-is-yet-to-come " side,
And the " fate-is-going-some " side
Any pessimist can see.

Kinder like to take my troubles,
Come they singly or in doubles,
As a boy does blowing bubbles,
In a hopeful sort of way;
Kinder like to look around them,
Sorter wistful like and sound them,
And eventually surround them,
'Till once more I 'm feeling gay.

Oh, this thing that 's known as worry,
That brings grouches in a hurry,
From your side will quickly scurry
If you keep a lifted chin;
If you 'll look your worries over,
Something cheerful you 'll discover,
You will get one breath of clover,
And once more you 'll wear a grin.

A Query ----

I wonder have you ever known
Or heard of such a thing
As paperhangers in the house
Who did n't try to sing?

OUT IN THE OPEN

OUT in the open, I long to be free,
Where the song that I hear is the song of the sea,
And the voice that I list to is soothing and sweet,
Away from the sound of the tramping of feet,
Not urging me ceaselessly into the fray,
Not spurring me ever to work when I 'd play;
Not picturing fame with its wealth and its power,
And the glory to be in my conquering hour,
But a voice that is tender and soothing and low,
That bids me to rest and to live as I go.

Out in the open, I long to be free,
To lazily dream in the shade of a tree,
To gaze into space where are pictures that soothe
Of life as a river, unruffled and smooth;
Not men at the forges, not men at the plows,
Not men winning wealth by the sweat of their brows,
Not men sore of muscle and weary of brain,
Unwilling to pause lest another should gain
The heights they are seeking, but men who can rest
And know that in living the dreaming is best.

Out in the open, I long to be free,
Away from the haunts of the glories to be,
To tune my poor soul to the song of a star,
And live for a while in the glories that are;
To rest when I 'm weary and drop from the strife,
Content with the blessings God gives us with life,
Not bound to the forge or the plow by a chain
That keeps men at work for the glory of gain,
No slave to the future, too frightened to rest,
But living the present and finding it blest.

JIMMY

I NEVER knew him, for he never grew
Up as so many strong little ones do;
Just a year on the earth with his mother, and then
God came and took Jimmy to heaven again.
And 't was years after that when I moved on the street
And met Jimmy's mother, so patient and sweet,
And through her I got to know Jimmy so well,
For morning and evening she 'd stop me to tell
About Jimmy.

His toys were all kept in his little play room,
His dolls and his Teddy bear stayed in the gloom;
And when Jimmy was two, or would have been, rather,
Some soldiers of tin were brought home by his father,
And the mother arranged them in battle line, too,
A fact that but few of her friends ever knew.
In her mind's eye she pictured him sunny and gay,
And often ceased work to romp with him and play,
Play with Jimmy.

In this way I got to know Jimmy myself,
Long after his toys had been put on the shelf;
He 'd been to school and to college, it seems,
And now was the man of his dear mother's dreams.
She 'd nursed him through measles and fevers and all
The ailments that everyone has when he 's small,
She'd lived with him, just as though he had been spared,
Played with him, prayed with him, worried and cared
For her Jimmy.

Wonderful, too, were the deeds he had done;
Never had mother before such a son.
Brave? Never youth was so fearless as he;

I 'm telling you now what she oft said to me.
And clever and witty and patient and kind,
With never a fault, but then mothers are blind,
And this mother really was telling the truth,
For she had watched every step of his youth,
Loving Jimmy.

The last words she spoke to me now I recall,
The doctor had whispered: "There 's no chance at all."
And she knew it, too, but she smiled up at me,
"I 'm going," she muttered, "my Jimmy to see,
I know how he looks, and I know what he 'll say,
For has n't he lived with me here every day?
Help father to bravely bear up under this,
For he will be lonesome, I know how he 'll miss
Me and Jimmy.

¶ Jealousy spoils more appetites than indigestion.

THE RIGHT FAMILY

WITH time our notions allus change,
An' years make old idees seem strange ---
Take Mary there --- time was when she
Thought one child made a family,
An' when our eldest, Jim, was born
She used t' say both night an' morn',
"One little one t' love an' keep,
T' guard awake, an' watch asleep,
T' bring up right an' lead him through
Life's paths is all we ought t' do."

Two years from then our Jennie came,
But Mary did n't talk the same;
"Now that 's just right," she said t' me,
"We 've got the proper family;
A boy an' girl, God sure is good,
It seems as though He understood
That I 've been hopin' every way
T' have a little girl some day;
Sometimes I 've prayed the whole night through ---
One ain't enough, we needed two."

Then as the months went rolling on,
One day the stork brought little John,
An' Mary smiled an' said t' me,
"The proper family is three;
Two boys, a girl t' romp an' play,
Jus' work enough t' fill the day.
I never had enough t' do,
The months that we had only two,
Three 's jus' right, pa, we do n't want more."
Still time went on an' we had four.

An' that was years ago, I vow,
An' we have six fine children now,
An' Mary 's plumb forgot the day
She used t' sit an' sweetly say
That one child was enough for her
T' love an' give the proper care;
Or two or three or four or five ---
Why, goodness gracious, sakes alive,
If God should send her ten t'night,
She 'd vow her fam'ly was jus' right!

THE HOMECOMER'S SONG

YE HO, for a sight of the land that I love,
And her flag floating high on the breeze;
Ye ho, for a sight of her blue skies above,
And the wonderful green of her trees!
For my heart 's beating now with expectancy's thrill,
And my eyes show the trace of a tear;
I love every river and valley and hill
In the land that I 've missed for a year.

Then it 's home once again,
Where the dear ones await,
And it 's back in the land of the free;
And it 's back once again
In my own native state,
This country 's the country for me.

The wonders of Egypt, the splendors of Rome,
And Italy's charms I have seen,
But my heart yearns today for the glories of home,
And the sight of my own native green.
For nowhere are skies e'er as tenderly blue,
Nor dews that so tenderly fall,
As here in the land of the free and the true,
The best land on earth after all.

Then it 's home once again,
Where the dear ones await,
And it 's back in the land of the free;
And it 's back once again
To my own native state,
This country 's the country for me.

O, nowhere on earth are there women so fair,
Or men quite so noble and brave;

O, nowhere are people less burdened with care
As here where the Stars and Stripes wave.
And nowhere do stars seem so brightly to shine,
Or trees seem to grow quite so tall,
As here in this country I hallow as mine,
The best land on earth after all.

Then it 's home once again,
Where the dear ones await,
And it 's back in the land of the free,
And it 's back once again
To my own native state,
This country 's the country for me.

MARK TWAIN

MARK TWAIN is dead! No, no, that cannot be,
Say rather Clemens knows life's mystery,
Say rather Clemens has been called above,
But Twain still lives for all the world to love.

Mark Twain is dead! 'T is false, I 'll not believe,
For Clemens only will I pause to grieve,
But Twain still lives, 't is Clemens passes by,
Mark Twain, Mark Twain was never born to die.

The hand that held the pen is nerveless now,
The chill of death rests coldly on his brow,
The voice that made us laugh will speak no more,
But Twain still lives to cheer us as before.

'T is Clemens who has torn the veil aside,
Who knows what is beyond the great divide,
'T is Clemens who is gone, who leaves behind
Mark Twain to cheer and comfort humankind.

AN ODE TO NELLIE

AH Nellie, you were always fair, and you were always good and true,
I 've sung about your wealth of hair, and praised your eyes, so soft and blue,
Your charms are many I confess, but now my pen in hand I take
To praise in my poor humble way the strawb'ry shortcake that you make.

It may be other maidens play a better bridge whist game than you,
That other wives for suffrage make far better speeches than you do,
And other women, it may be, know more of Browning and of Keats,
But you make shortcake, Nellie dear, that every other woman's beats.

And were you lacking in those charms that cheer the eye and warm the heart,
Were you not fair to look upon --- an angel's very counterpart ---
Were you not gentle, patient, kind, did you not soothe my every ache,
I still should love you, Nellie, for the strawb'ry shortcake that you make.

¶ The other fellow is no happier than you are, his job is no easier than yours, his troubles are just as great, and altogether he is traveling along in the same old path; and you are only wasting time when you sit and envy him.

ROSES, BIRDS AND SOME MEN

THE world is full of roses, blooming red for me and you,
They smile a morning welcome and are wet with heavenly dew,
And every oak and maple, and every apple thorn
Have a song bird on their branches singing gayly in the morn;
But you never see a red rose waiting in a cloud of gloom
For some one who will coax it and persuade it into bloom,
And you never see a song bird sitting idly in a tree
In a solemn, sullen manner till one begs for melody.

No, the red rose blooms in sweetness and it gives its charms to all,
And the bees may sip its honey, and the honey 's never gall;
E'en a little child may pluck it, or a mother old and gray,
For the rose's special mission is to glad some heart each day.
And the song bird in the branches just as sweetly trills and sings
For the ploughboys in the furrows as he would for mighty kings.
O, there never was a red rose or a song bird up above,
That you had to beg for favors or you had to know to love.

But with men it 's O, so different, there are some who smile and sing
And scatter love and sunshine, like the song birds on the wing,

But we find too oft a mortal who could make his brothers glad,
Sitting solemnly and grimly, with a visage long and sad,
Waiting some one who will coax him, who will flatter for his smile,
Ere he 'll sing a song of gladness or do anything worth while.
Give me men with gifts who use them, and who let their spirits flow,
One is worth a dozen mortals whom to like you have to know.

TWO VIEWPOINTS

OUT in the open, the wide sky above,
And the green meadows stretched at my feet;
Out in the open, midst scenes that I love,
Where the rest hour is soothing and sweet;
Out in the country, where nature 's at play
And the wild flowers look up with a smile,
I am hurrying now for a short holiday,
I am going to rest there a while.

Into the city, where life is n't dead,
An' there 's something a feller can do;
Where hundreds of people keep forging ahead
An' runnin' right plump into you;
Where there 's hustle an' bustle, an' something to see,
An' you never get lonesome nor blue;
I tell you, the city 's the fine place to be,
An' I 'm goin' when ploughin' is through.

THE TRAGEDY OF AGE

I HEARD an old man say today:
"A young man gives me orders now,"
A beardless youth gets better pay
And tells me what to do and how;
While I have toiled for forty years,
A stripling enters in the race
And with a single bound appears
And eagerly usurps my place.

"I 've seen them shake their heads at me,
And I have often heard them sigh
As they my faltering hand would see:
'The times, alas, have passed him by,
He is n't what he used to be,
He 's lost his grip,' and well I knew
That youth at last had conquered me,
As youth old age will ever do.

"And now it 's come, and I behold
Young fighters stripped to face the fray,
Exultant, clear of eye and bold,
Where I was wont to lead the way.
My nerve, they say, is gone from me,
I fear to do what youth will dare,
I shrink from opportunity,
My place is in an easy chair.

"This has been so since time began,
And to the end of time will be,
Brief is the working time of man,
Brief as the leaf upon the tree.
The young man comes, the old man goes,
Old eyes, old brains, old bodies fail,
Beyond our powers the struggle grows,
Old age drops out. So ends the tale."

WHEN THE DRESSMAKER COMES

WHEN the dressmaker comes I am told to clear out,
For they do n't want me anywhere hanging about;
At seven in the morning they send me away
With: " Do n't you come back till the close of the day;
She 'll be here for a week, and we 've so much to do
That we can't afford to be bothered by you.
So get up and dress,
Eat your breakfast in less
Than a jiffy! She 's coming today --- clear the track!
Here 's your hat. Now, good-bye;
Move along and be spry,
You must hurry away, but, O, do n't hurry back."

When the dressmaker comes every room in the place
Is littered with patterns and trimmings and lace;
There are snippings and cuttings from parlor to kitchen,
And stuff on each bed that the women are stitchin';
And never a chair from the time they begin it,
But is sure to have needles and pins sticking in it.
And always they say,
At the coming of day:
" Get up and get out just as quick as you can,
Hurry up now, Skiddoo!
This is no place for you,
When the dressmaker 's here we can't fuss with a man.

When the dressmaker comes I am driven from home;
They hand me my hat and command me to roam,
And the meals they do get would arouse Dr. Wiley,
The chops are half cooked and the coffee is " riley,"
And all through the week not a kind word is said
Unto me from the morn 'till I sneak up to bed.

With a mouth full of pins
Thus my darling begins:
"Can't you see we are busy? We 've no time for you,
Goodness gracious, please go,
You 're delaying us so,
And please do n't come back till the dressmaker 's through."

FISHIN'- HUNGER

BLUE skies mighty temptin', an' the sunbeams coaxin', too,
An' my wo'k is gettin' harder ebery day;
Ain't a-takin' any int'rest in de things I has t' do,
Jes' sittin' heah an' wishin' time away.
Jes' a-wishin' fo' de fishin'
An' de wet line gayly swishin'
As I fling it t' de middle o' de stream,
An' I let it drif' and dribble,
Till I feel de pick'rel nibble,
Dat 's de burden o' my everlastin' dream.

Dere is some folks call it hook worm, an' dere 's others say dat I
Am jes' nacherly inclined t' laziness;
An' I aint a-goin' t' quarrel or dispute or argufy,
It 's de fishin'-hunger 's got me though, I guess.
Jes' de fishin'-hunger schemin'
An' a-keepin' of me dreamin'
An' a-lurin' me out yonder t' de bay
Where de pick'rel am playin'
An' de willow trees am swayin',
It 's de fishin'-hunger makes me act dis way.

THE NEIGHBORS

WHY do I grind from morn till night,
And sick or well sit down to write?
Why do I line my brow with sweat,
An extra buck or two to get?
The reason is n't hard to trace,
For us our neighbors set the pace.

The Greens go weekly to a show,
And so, of course, we have to go;
A dollar-fifty per they pay
For seats down in the parquet,
And always they wear evening dress;
We could n't think of doing less.

The Browns maintain a servant girl,
The one we have was christened Pearl;
At dinner, several kinds of wine
They serve in glass of rare design.
Their dinners are a great success;
And ours, of course, must be no less.

In summer all our neighbors flee
Unto the mountains or the sea;
They spend two months in big hotels
And hobnob with the other swells;
And though it 's costly, I confess
That wife of mine shall do no less.

Two doors from us lives Mrs. Grout,
Who owns a lovely runabout,
And though she 's very nice, it 's plain
She looks on us with some disdain.
Although it 's more than I can do,
My wife will shortly have one, too.

I 'd like to take a holiday
And spend a month or two in play;
I 'd like to take an ocean trip
And give this awful grind the slip;
But there 's no rest for me the while
We let our neighbors set the style.

NOTHING UNUSUAL

THEY lived together thirty years,
Through storm and sunshine, weal and woe;
They shared each other's hopes and fears ---
She still his sweetheart, he her beau;
She, proud of him, though he was not
A millionaire, or known to fame.
The wife --- contented with her lot,
The man --- well, very much the same.

He never thought she ought to be
Always agreeable and gay;
And she did not expect that he
Would never have a grouchy day.
She did not think that he was one
Without a single fault or whim,
Nor did she try a paragon
Of goodness to make out of him.

But, hand in hand, they went along
Through all the moods that humans know;
Displeasure came when things went wrong,
She still his sweetheart, he her beau.
Frowns, smiles, delight, despair, they knew,
With love always to dry their tears,
Just simple human folks, those two
Who lived together thirty years.

THE WORRY - CHASER

COME here to me, little lassie of three,
And get in your place on your old daddy's knee,
Put those chubby arms round where they nightly belong
And cling to my neck, for the day has gone wrong
And I need you, I need you to scatter away
All the cares and the griefs of a troublesome day.

Let 's sing the old songs and the old lullabies
Till the light of joy burns once again in my eyes;
Let 's ride up to London at doublefast trot
Till all of my worries and cares are forgot;
Let 's romp on the floor and make merry tonight,
For you, little girl, can put everything right.

You tickle my ribs and I 'll tickle your toes,
You tug at my beard and I 'll tug at your nose,
I 'll blow down your neck and you blow down mine,
Then we 'll ride pig-a-back and do everything fine;
And the first thing I know I 'll be gay and care-free,
Come, little lassie, climb onto my knee.

I was cross, I was mean, through the heat of the day,
I gave up to despair as my plans went astray;
But it 's all over now, and I want to forget
The troubles that caused me to worry and fret.
And you are my sunshine, my source of delight,
So come to your dad and make everything right!

Unphilosophic ----

Let philosophers say that it 's all for the best
No matter what happens awry,
I defy one to smile who spills pie on his vest,
Especially loose pumpkin pie.

CONSOLATION

SO YOU 'RE sobbin' in the night time, an' you 're
sighin' through the day,
An' your heart is ever callin' for the loved one gone away;
An' you 're lonely, oh, so lonely! an' there 's nothin'
friends can do,
That will start the old light shinin' in those tender
eyes of blue.

I 'm not goin' to try to tell you that you should n't sit
an' sigh,
An' I 'm not the one to whisper: "You 'll feel better
by an' by;"
But joy is n't everlastin' till this earthly life is done,
If it was, no cloud would ever hide the shinin' mornin'
sun.

We must sip of joy an' sorrow, we must weep an'
laugh in turn,
We must win love but to lose it, an' our hearts with
grief must burn;
For the lasting joys are Heaven's, we can't hope to
find them here,
Every one who loves must some day weep beside a
loved one's bier.

To have known love an' deserved it, is our highest
point of bliss,
There 's no happiness for mortals that can greater be
than this;
An' though Death comes in an' robs us of our priceless
jewels, we
Who have loved an' lost know something of the joys
that are to be.

TODAY

TODAY is mine. Tomorrow may not come.
Next week, next year, I may not live to see;
This hour I have. It is enough for me
To make by smiles, or mar by being glum.
And so I strive to live this one day well,
To tread the path of right as best I may,
To speak the kind words that I have to say;
Tomorrow I may be an empty shell.

One day is all God gives to us to plan,
And so I strive to live it as my life,
To bear with patience what I find of strife,
To do my share to cheer my fellow man;
To do today what I can do to aid,
To let none pass whom words of mine might cheer,
Tomorrow they may not be toiling here,
Tomorrow in the ground I may be laid.

¶ Faint heart ne'er got an oleander up the cellar steps, either.

DO YOU?

YOU pay what you owe to your neighbor, I know,
You do the square thing by your brother,
Your word is as good in your own neighborhood
As the bond or the cash of another.
With promptness you pay all your bills on the day
They are due, with a check or the pelf,
But let me inquire, when alone by the fire,
Do you ever square up with yourself?

Do you ever sit down, when you 've come from the town,
And sum up your work for the day?
Do you look over all, both the big and the small,
And check them and file them away?
Are you honest with "you" in all things that you do,
Do your credits and debits agree?
With your neighbors you 're fair, but are you on the square
With yourself as you really should be?

Say, young man! Look here! Are you really sincere;
Are you honestly doing your best?
Are you bluffing your way, or prepared any day
For life to put you to the test?
Are you sure of your ground, are your principles sound,
Are your purposes honest and true?
Paying bills as you go is a good sign, I know,
But how do you square up with "you"?

There 's a debt that you owe to yourself. Is it paid?
An account of your own that is due;
"As good as your word" is a phrase often heard,
Would your conscience repeat it of you?
Your grocer may dwell on your promptness and tell
How you pay for the goods on his shelf;
But think you today that your conscience would say
That you 're honest and square with yourself?

Can't Frighten Them ----

This is the way to take your woes,
Just grin and bear 'em,
Since everybody round here knows
A frown won't scare 'em.

SOME DAY

SOME day our eyes will brighten, and some day
our hearts will lighten,
Some day the sun will shine for you and me;
Some day grim doubt we 'll banish, and the clouds of
woe will vanish,
And the rosy, golden future we shall see.
Some day we 'll know the wherefore of earth's journey,
sweetheart, therefore
Let us bear the present bravely as we go,
Let us sing our songs of gladness, though our hearts
are tinged with sadness,
We shall some day reach the valley where the
roses bloom and blow.

Some day in the hereafter we shall find the will for
laughter,
And the smiles will deck our faces once again;
And upon that brighter morrow, you shall ne'er have
cause for sorrow,
For I 'll never stay out later, dear, than ten;
Some day I 'll cease to worry you while dressing, or to
hurry you,
But patiently I 'll wait until you come,
And though late we are, my dearie, I shall still be gay
and cheery,
On the day when little trials shall have ceased to
make us glum.

Some day soon, I feel it coming, when the bees once
more are humming,
And the snows have melted silently away,
When the skies above are tender, and old Mother Earth
in splendor

Bedecks herself with pansies and the tulips red
and gay,
Maybe somebody will write me and in pleasant terms
invite me
To spend Sunday at his cottage on the bay;
And that day when we are fishing, and our lines are
gayly swishing,
We shall never have to murmur that the big ones
got away.

¶ It is n't a man's purse, but his personality that counts.

HIS CHANCE

"I WANT a chance to show what I can do,"
He sighed when others seemed to pass him by;
"There are great problems I could master, too,
Somehow, I never get the chance to try.

"Give me a chance to show what I can do,"
This was the burden of his daily whine;
"I might achieve success as well as you,
If opportunity were mine."

One day they bade him fill another's place,
Another's work they offered him to do;
He grumbled and a frown passed o'er his face,
"I am not paid to do the work of two."

THEY 'RE COMING BACK

THEY 'RE coming home Thanksgiving Day,
They 're coming back once more,
And mother's smiles begin to play
The way they did before
The youngsters went away. Somehow
She does n't seem so old;
The lines have faded from her brow,
She 's sprightly now and bold.
And yesterday she sang a song
That took me back to when
The youngest merely crept along,
And Frank was only ten.

They 're coming home Thanksgiving Day,
And mother shows it, too;
Her hair, somehow, is not so gray,
And in her eyes the blue
Is clearer than it used to be,
And in them there 's a light
Of love that I was wont to see
When courting her at night.
She 's singing songs again, and in
Her voice there 's not a crack,
Once more the dimple 's in her chin,
For they are coming back.

They 're coming back, that 's all we know,
They 're coming back to see
The mother of the long ago,
They 're coming back to me.
And we 've put off a thousand woes,
And shelved a dozen years;

In mother's fading cheek the rose
Of June once more appears;
The old home seems to thrill once more
The way it used to, when
The baby crept along the floor
And Frank was only ten.

THE LILACS

I ALWAYS think of mother, when
The lilac tree 's in bloom,
It seems her soul comes back again
Upon its sweet perfume.
And every opal spire that sways
Out in the summer sun
Brings back the good old golden days
Before her work was done.

'T was there her smile seemed sweetest, and
'T was there her eyes were brightest,
'T was there that gentlest was her hand,
And there her heart was lightest.
And now when blooms the lilac tree
I feel that she is near me,
Come back again the flowers to see,
To comfort and to cheer me.

All mothers love a lilac tree,
And that is why I love it;
The blossoms know, it seems to me,
That angels bend above it.
And when the blooms return again
My skies become the clearest,
Because I seem to feel just then
That mother, dear, is nearest.

A LITTLE THE BEST OF IT

A LITTLE the best of it,
Allus he prayed for,
All th' time lookin'
Fer more than he paid for,
Had an idee, that 's
What bargains are made for.

Whatever he sold,
Folks made up their minds to it,
He got th' best of it,
Everyone knew it,
There warn't any trick
Known, but what he could do it.

Sand in th' sugar,
His thumb on the scales,
Short weight in flour
An' ten-penny nails,
Made his own lard,
An' he weighed in th' pails.

Bet when he dies,
An' he makes a clean breast of it,
Tells good St. Peter
His yarn, with the rest of it,
He 'll make a plea
For a little th' best of it.

¶ You can make good by doing your work just a little bit better than it was ever done before. There may be other ways, but up to date they have n't been discovered.

THE SWEETEST SOUL I EVER KNEW

THE sweetest soul I ever knew
Had suffered untold sorrow,
Had wept full many a long night through
And feared the dark tomorrow.
Oh! she had seen her baby die
And seen her loved ones taken,
Full many a tear had dimmed her eye,
But her faith remained unshaken.

Her hair was white as the driven snow,
And her brow with care was lined,
But all untouched by the years of woe
Was the sweetness of her mind;
And all unharmed by the years of care
And the dreary nights of grieving
Was the gentle smile of that woman fair,
Still trustful, still believing.

Joy never produces a soul like this,
They come from the fires of anguish,
This perfect sweetness of mind they miss,
Who in rose-red bowers languish;
For out of the heartache and out of pain
And the suffering unabated,
The shattered hopes that were held in vain,
Was this wonderful soul created.

¶ A fresh young man and a profane old man are two horribly false notes in this otherwise harmonious world scheme.

MEMORIAL DAY

BRING your roses to the valley
Where in dreamless sleep they lie
Never more on earth to rally
'Round the flag that waves on high.
Spread your roses on the waters
Where they slumber 'neath the wave,
We are heroes' sons and daughters,
We are mourners for the brave.

Do you think they are forgotten
Just because they nameless lie
Where the swaying fields of cotton
Point their bolls up to the sky?
Or because the waves are keeping
Restless vigil o'er the spot
Where today in death they 're sleeping,
Do you think that we 've forgot?

While our little ones are playing
In the gentle summer sun,
And their little feet are straying
Where the paths of childhood run,
With the flag of freedom flying
In the blue skies overhead,
Would you say that mem'ry 's dying
Of our sainted hero dead?

While our men are self denying
And our women pure and true,
While brave hearts are ever trying
For the good that they can do;
While the love of freedom lingers
In a single human breast,
One shall deck with tender fingers
Graves where heroes are at rest.

For on nameless graves is founded,
    And from nameless tombs has sprung
Blessed freedom, to be sounded
    By each patriotic tongue.
And the greatness of our nation
    And the peace that now we know,
Have for their secure foundation
    These, our dead of Long Ago.

¶ Where there 's a will, you can always find interested relatives.

AT THE COTTAGE

SHE wanted to be asked again,
    And so she wiped the dishes,
She took a knife, and with the men
    She helped to clean the fishes;
She made her bed and swept the floor,
    She ran for water gayly,
She tackled every menial chore,
    And pared potatoes daily.

She wanted to be asked again,
    She ran to do the shopping,
She toiled from early morn till ten
    And never thought of stopping;
She got the meals and met the boat,
    She really was a hummer,
By diligence, I 'd have you note,
    She earned a pleasant summer.

LITTLE MISS SIX O'CLOCK

JUST at the edge of the night and the morning,
Little Miss Six O'clock comes to my bed,
A sweet little laugh is her musical warning
That day time is here and the night time is fled.
And I am so sleepy, and I am so weary,
I want to doze on for an hour or two more,
But Little Miss Six O'clock, bright-eyed and cheery,
Has come to announce that the sleep time is o'er.

Little Miss Six O'clock, that 's what I call her,
As brim full of fun as a rose is of dew;
And as sweet as a rose, only plumper and taller,
Comes to announce that the night time is through.
Smiles that are brighter than May sunbeams dancing
Already out there on the velvety lawn,
Over the counterpane bounding and prancing,
Little Miss Six O'clock heralds the morn.

" Wake up, lazy daddy! wake up, it is day time! "
She shouts in my ear as she tickles my nose,
" Wake up, lazy daddy! it 's morning and play time! "
Then she tickles my ribs with her little pink toes.
For a minute or more I pretend to be sleeping,
Till over her face comes the trace of a pout,
And Little Miss Six O'clock shows signs of weeping,
Then " O, my goodness, is that you? " I shout.

We bounce and we roll and bump and jump,
And under the covers I hide away,
And I pretend I 'm an old tree stump
Out in the woods where the fairies play.
I 've forgotten that I was a tired old dad
Who wanted to sleep, and I 'm trouble free;
And every morning my heart is glad
When Little Miss Six O'clock comes to me.

OUT OF THE DAY

OUT of the day you have taken what,
Crown of laurels and wreath of bay?
Smiles or frowns? Did you bring away
Shame that stings like an iron hot,
Or did you close with a record fair?
Out of the day you have taken what,
Peace of mind or a night of care?

Sum it all up as you close the page,
What have you written throughout the day,
Joy or sorrow? Be honest, say
Evil wrought in an hour of rage,
Wrongs that loom through the dead of night?
Sum it all up as you close the page,
Fair or foul are the things you write?

Over your record muse with care,
And note the wrong that is written down;
Why this temper and why this frown?
You were the one to put them there,
You were the one to stoop to sin;
Over your record muse with care,
Yours is the fault if you failed to win.

Out of the day you have taken what,
Joy or sorrow? Then let me ask
What brought you to your daily task?
A cheerful mind with your woes forgot,
Or an air of gloom with a downcast chin?
Out of the day you have taken what?
Merely the fruits of what you put in.

THE FIGHT WITH SELF

WE ALL have fights to make with self,
And these are the bitterest fights of all,
Worse than the fight for a hoard of pelf
Is the fight to master our vices small;
Worse than the fight on the battle line
Is the struggle that many a man goes through
To rid himself of the thirst for wine,
That he may live as he wants to do.

Temptation knocks at the good priest's door,
And fierce is the struggle within his breast,
But he kneels and prays till the siege is o'er
And rises a victor in the test.
And man and woman must fight as he
The things of self that would drag us down,
And over ourselves get the mastery
Else all we gain is a paper crown.

Oh, the fight for wealth and the fight for fame,
The fight for glory and world applause;
The struggle, too, for an honored name,
And I 'd list the fight for a noble cause,
Are simple things, if the truth were known,
Compared to the struggle a man goes through
In his fight with self, when he 's all alone,
To live a life that is clean and true.

¶ A man has made a big stride toward popularity when he has come to the point where he can recognize that the other fellow is as much entitled to enjoy life as he is.

THE WAY TO DO

"HOW 'S things? says I,
  Says he " Not bad,
They might be worse,
  But then I 'm glad
They ain't." That 's all
  He had to say,
An' whistled as
  He went away.

He had his troubles,
  That I knew,
And sorrows also
  Grieved him, too.
But not a word
  Of them, says he,
But kep' 'em to
  Himself, you see.

" How 's things? " says I,
  " Not bad," says he,
" They might be worse,"
  An' seems to me,
That 's jes' the thing
  We all should say
About our troubles
  Every day.

They might be worse,
  Of course they might.
This thought should put
  Our gloom to flight.
Let 's cease our
  Troubles to rehearse,
And tell our friends
  They might be worse.

MY PLAN

WHEN I wanted something I could n't buy,
A suit of clothes or a Sunday tie,
Or a new straw hat when the sun was high,
I used to feel sore about it.
I used to go 'round with a face drawn long,
And vow that everything here was wrong,
And this was the theme of my dismal song,
I can't get along without it.

When I 've been broke, which has oft occurred,
I never could utter a cheerful word,
I grouched all day, which was most absurd,
And kicked up a fuss about it.
I thought what I wanted and could n't get
Was reason enough to fume and fret,
So I fretted and fumed all day, and yet
I managed to do without it.

Now whatever I want that I cannot buy,
A suit of clothes or a Sunday tie,
Or a new straw hat when the sun is high,
I do n't say a word about it.
I 've found that my wants need n't interfere
With my daily fun on this hemisphere,
What I can't afford does n't spoil my cheer,
I just get along without it.

Slangy ----

There was a young woman named Strong,
Much given to slang, which is wrong;
When the grave parson said:
" Will this man you now wed? "
She said: " Sure Mike! That 's why he 's along."

LOOKING BACK

LOOKIN' back, I think I see,
Folks who thought a heap of me,
Folks who used to shout my praise,
Help me, too, along life's ways,
Cheer me up when I was blue,
Share my little sorrows, too,
Knew me well before I came
Here to make myself a name.

Wonder where they are today,
Wonder if they ever say
Kind words of me, now as then,
Dear old women, good old men;
Often now I blush for shame,
In the rush for gold and fame
From them I have turned away.
Wonder where they are today?

Have they quite forgotten me?
Would they know me, could they see
Me once more, and would they say
Those kind words of yesterday?
O, that I could journey back,
Over life's wide, boundless track,
All their kindness I'd repay
In a better, sweeter way.

I'd not drift away as I
Now have drifted; I would try
To remember them and be
Still with them in memory.
I would try to know that they
Talked of me from day to day;
Never would I wondering be
Have old friends forgotten me.

MEN AND THE DREAMERS

IT 'S one o' my idees that men ain't all of fightin' stock,
They ain't all built fer ploughin' or fer hewin' out a rock;
An' they ain't all made fer battlin' up against life's steady stream,
There must be some of us on earth God put here jes' to dream;
Leastwise it strikes me that way --- if it was n't so, I guess,
Instead o' dreamin' here I 'd be out hustlin' fer success.

There 's men that 's fond o' money and there 's men in love with fame,
An' there 's others seekin' glory an' a great an' honored name;
There 's men that 's built fer fightin', men who love to plan an' scheme,
Men that 's born with love o' conquest, an' there 's men that love to dream;
Men who 'd rather spend a life time where the roses bloom and nod
Than win prizes on the highways where the fightin' brothers plod.

Folks may call me shiftless, maybe, an' may sneer when they go by
In their autos big an' splendid, while I 'm gazin' at the sky,
An' perhaps they think I envy 'em the luxuries they know.
But I do n't. My soul do n't need 'em, an' I 'd gladly tell 'em so.

Fer I 'm happier with the roses, an' the hollyhocks
an' trees
Than I would be makin' money --- that is why I take
my ease.

¶ The knocker can always get an audience, but he seldom gets an encore.

SYMPATHY

ONE came to the house with a pretty speech,
"It 's all for the best," said he,
And I know that he sought my heart to reach,
And I know that he grieved with me.

But I was too full of my sorrow then
To list to his words or care;
Though I 've tried I cannot recall again
The comfort he gave me there.

But another came, and his lips were dumb,
As he grasped me by the hand,
And he stammered: "Old man, I had to come,
O, I hope you 'll understand."

And ever since then I have felt his hand
Clasped tightly in my own,
And today his silence I understand ---
My sorrowing he had known.

THE SUMMER ARGUMENT

SHE wants to go unto the shore,
And pack her trunk
With gowns no one has seen before,
And all such junk.

But I would seek some far off place
Where I 'm unknown,
And let my whiskers deck my face,
And be alone.

She sighs for parties and for teas,
They are her wish;
I merely want to take my ease
And loaf and fish.

She wants to lead a life that 's grand,
In silken skirts;
I want to wear old trousers and
My outing shirts.

True Philosophy ----

I would n't count it worth my while
To sing about a rich man's smile,
Or quote a fellow, trouble free,
An' label that philosophy.

But when I look about and find
A cripple or a brother blind,
An' hear him singing songs of glee,
I want that man's philosophy.

THE FARMER TALKS

HERE 's a letter from John in th' city,
Ain't heard from him now fer a year;
Yes, his handwritin' s stylish an' pretty,
An' rounded an' wonderf'ly clear;
Says he hopes we are all well an' thrivin',
Remarks that June 's been rather cool,
But I know jes' at what he is drivin'
When he says that the kids have done school.

Do n't hear much from John through the winter,
Excep' when I go into town,
An' then he do n't even begin ter
Warm up or git rid of his frown;
Guess he ain't fond of much entertainin',
An' mebbe thinks I am a fool,
Yet, I know jes' why he 's explainin'
The kids will be soon out of school.

Poor John ain't got much excep' trouble,
A mortgage or two an' some debts.
An' I sell a hog fer jes' double
The weekly amount that he gets;
But still John is given ter braggin',
In the city that 's often the rule;
An' his wife is eternally naggin'---
So the kids will be soon out of school.

Well, I guess that I 'll send fer 'em, Jenny,
Though I ain't got much use fer John,
An' I would n't favor him any,
But now that th' summer is on,
Those youngsters need sunshine, I 'm thinkin',
An' air that is fresh an' is cool;
I 'm writin' him --- darn me, I 'm blinkin'---
To send 'em when they 're out of school.

A SONG

I'M never too weary to sing you a song.
I 'm never too weary to play,
For here on my knee, little one, you belong
And here on my knee you may stay;
The day may be bitter and dreary and sad,
But the night time shall ever be gay,
In spite of the worries and troubles I 've had,
I 'm never too weary to play.

So, up on my knee for a fairy tale now
Of the prince and the wonderful maid,
The prince with the curls hanging over his brow,
The girl with her hair in a braid;
We'll follow the youth to the tower and we'll see
How he battles the bold wicked men
Who are holding her there,'till at last she is free
And the bad king is killed in his den.

I 'm never too weary to tell you a tale,
I 'm never too weary, my dear
To conjure up stories from meadow and vale,
And the dwarf with the comical ear;
For worn though I am by the city's pell-mell,
On my knee, little one, you belong,
Forever my lips have a story to tell,
And my heart strings are tuned for a song.

¶ If opportunity only made a noise like a dinner bell when she called, perhaps more men would respond.

TO THE FAILURES

YOURS is the loser's part to play,
For you the goal is far away
And never to be gained.
It is your lot to stand and see
The golden apples on life's tree
By some one else attained;
To view with yearning in your eyes
Another grasp the precious prize.

It is for you to wade through fire,
To feel the burning of desire
And want unsatisfied;
And from the sleepless hours of night
You rise at morn, once more to fight
With victory denied;
Spurred on by hope that never dies,
You struggle ever toward the prize.

A failure? Yes, as glory goes,
Yet braver in the end than those
Who life's great battles win;
For you return at break of day
With courage to renew the fray,
And with a lifted chin
You strive once more to reach the goal,
And ground your bark upon a shoal.

But when earth's story shall be told,
And God's great purpose we behold
With eyes new-born to see;
When we have passed beyond the pale
Of earth, and torn aside the veil
Of death's great mystery,
As souls victorious you 'll stand
And God's great prizes you 'll command.

RATHER STAY HOME

NEVER so happy as when I 'm at home,
I 'm not so anxious to wander or roam;
Rather sit down with the folks who love me,
With somebody's youngster astride of my knee,
And gallop him off to the wonderful land,
Where armies are waiting his word to command,
Than listen to speeches by eloquent men
Who shout for an hour and then sit down again.

Never so happy as when I 'm at home,
Rather play tunes with a paper and comb
For a boy or a girl who may drop in to call,
For it 's there that I shine if I do shine at all;
Rather sing ditties to tots that I know,
Than go to a party or go to a show,
Or listen to grown-ups with wisdom expound,
As their arms saw the air, and the tables they pound.

Never so happy as when I 'm at home,
Do n't care to journey to Naples or Rome,
Rather stay here with the folks who love me,
Than run after strangers whoever they be;
A nod from a king or a smile from a lord
Would n't please me a bit. I 'd be terribly bored;
Rather stay here where I 'm loved and I 'm known,
Than get on my knees before any old throne.

¶ Learn to be patient with others and to so conduct yourself that others won't find it necessary to be patient with you.

After a June bride has seen the same pay envelope for a few weeks she begins to wonder why there is n't more in it.

THE SONGS OF NIGHT

THE moon swings low in the sky above,
And the twinkling stars shine bright,
And a mother sings to her baby love
Those wonderful songs of night;
Those wonderful songs of sugar plum trees,
And the fields where the fairies play,
Of cockle-shell boats on golden seas
That never are seen by day.

It is by-low time and she sweetly hums
Those wonderful songs of night;
Of the blare of trumpets and sound of drums
When the little tin soldiers fight;
She sings of a comical candy dog
And the gingerbread man who stands
By the side of a blinking cooky frog,
Without any arms or hands.

And the moonbeams dance on the parlor floor,
And a ship sets out to sea,
And a baby sails for the golden shore
In search of the sugar plum tree;
She 's off to the cave of the Teddy Bear,
And the haunts of the fairies kind,
Where never an ache or a pain or care
Shall trouble her baby mind.

Oh, sweet is the smile on the baby's face
As she softly sinks to rest,
For where in the world is so fine a place
To sleep, as a mother's breast?
And if ever a song can reach the skies,
The angels must find delight
In hearing a mother's lullabies ---
Those wonderful songs of night.

EASTER

OUT of the darkness and shadow of death,
Out of the anguish that wells from the tomb,
Into the splendor of spiritual breath,
Now we have burst like a lily in bloom;
Sweetened is sorrow and strengthened is hope,
Death and the grave have been robbed of their sting;
Doubting, despairing, no longer we grope,
Man has been given the courage to sing.

Easter! the birthday of hope and of peace!
Easter! the bulwark of all we believe;
Lo, all our wailings and sad moanings cease,
Death has been shorn of its power to grieve.
See! now a mother, her cheeks wan and white,
Smilingly sinks into slumber most blest;
Her soul unto Heaven is borne through the night,
And she wakes in the morn with her babe at her breast.

Look! from a newly made grave comes a man,
Feeble and bowed by the struggles of life,
"She waits for my coming," he says, "and the span
Is but short for me now to the side of my wife.
Though I miss her, I mourn not her going, I know
That she is at rest, and far happier there;
And I wait but the summons when I am to go
To the valley of peace, from the land of despair."

And this is the meaning of Easter's glad songs,
And this is the reason that Easter is gay;
"He is risen," we sing, "He has righted earth's wrongs,
From the mouth of the tomb see the stone rolled away."

Yes, out of the darkness and gloom of the tomb,
He has risen, our Master, our Lord and our King!
And we view not life's end as a signal of doom,
But the birth of new life, and we 've courage to sing.

THE BOY MIND

WISH I was only as bright as my boy,
Wish I could think of the things that he springs;
His is a wit without any alloy,
His are real jokes without venomous stings.
Laugh? When he speaks, from the tip of your toes
To the top of your head you will shake through and through,
As the soft breeze of summer oft shakes the red rose,
And the petals of pansies are thrilled by the dew.

Wish I was only as bright as my boy,
Wish I could think of such funny remarks,
His little mind is a fountain of joy,
Throwing off fun as an anvil sheds sparks.
He makes us laugh if we want to or not,
Never was jester of king quite so droll,
His are the shafts that go right to the spot,
His is a humor that tickles your soul.

None of the quips that your funny men say
Is equal to those that the child mind produces;
He has the power to drive sorrow away,
The flood gates of laughter he gayly unlooses.
Wise? As the wisest of brow wrinkled sages;
Quaint? As the quaintest of men on the earth;
Funny? Why, none of your funniest pages
Compare with a boy for real laughter and mirth.

HIS PHILOSOPHY

JIM had a quaint philosophy,
"It ain't fer you, it 's jes' fer me,"
He used to say. "I do n't p'tend
T' force it onto foe or friend;
I do n't advise or recommend
This way or that fer him nor you,
Or try t' tell you what t' do;
But I jes' take myself aside
An' teach him tricks he 's never tried.

"I kinder take myself in hand
An' try t' make him understand
That he must do a full day's work,
An' ain't got time t' loaf an' shirk;
An' when he gets a load of care,
His shoulders are the ones t' bear
That burden, not his neighbors or
Some friend he might go running for.

"I try t' teach myself t' smile,
T' whistle every little while,
T' take whatever comes his way
As his just portion of th' day;
An' not complain an' fume an' frown,
An' vow th' world is runnin' down
An' ragged at th' heel becoz
Things ain't as pleasant as they was.

"Fer I 've got all that I can do
T' keep myself in line; that 's true.
It ain't fer me t' stand up now
An' try t' tell my neighbors how
They ought t' live, an' what t' do,
T' hold up all their faults t' view.

Reformin' others may be fine,
But somehow that ain't in my line.

" Yes, I 've my own philosophy,
But it 's intended jes' fer me;
It 's made t' keep myself in line,
T' make me never show a sign
Of fear or cowardice when things
Go wrong or untold sorrow stings,
An' that is all that I can do ---
You 'll have t' say what 's best fer you."

WINDS OF THE MORNING

WINDS of the morning, whisper low,
Lingered you in the valley where
Sleeps my love of the Long Ago,
Under the pale green grasses there?

Tell me, winds of the morning, sweet,
There you paused in your gentle way,
Before you came to the city street,
To kiss the daisies that o'er her sway.

There, from there, all your fragrance rare
You gathered, winds of the morning, say;
Whisper low that you come from there
To cheer the heart of me today.

Winds of the morning, so cool and sweet,
Laden with fragrance; I know, I know
You have come from that deep retreat,
Where sleeps my love of the Long Ago.

THE RICH MAN'S WOES

HE 'S worth a million dollars and you think he should be glad,
Because you want for money you believe he can't be sad;
His name is in the papers nearly every day or so,
If he wants a trip to Europe he can pack his grip and go,
But he 's really heavy-hearted and he often wears a frown,
For his daughter contradicts him and his new wife calls him down.

He 's not dunned by bill collectors, and he does n't have to fret
Though the cost of living 's soaring; what he wants he 's sure to get.
He can order from his tailor three or four suits at a time,
And he tips the waiters dollars where another tips a dime;
But he really is n't happy as he motors round the town,
For his daughter contradicts him and his new wife calls him down.

O, it 's folly to sit yearning for another fellow's lot,
For he 's sure to have some worries that perhaps afflict you not;
And it 's folly now to wish for any other fellow's place,
For it 's certain he has troubles that would make you sour of face;
And the man who 's worth a million maybe wants to be a clown
When his daughter contradicts him and his new wife calls him down.

THE JOYS OF EARTH

LAUGHTER and song and mirth,
Roses that drip with dew,
These are the joys of earth;
Sunshine and skies of blue,
Children that romp and play,
Stars that twinkle at night,
Moonbeams that softly stray
Making the meadows light.

Birds in the tree tops high,
Fish in the waters blue,
Rain from the summer sky,
Sweethearts whose love is true;
Mountains and hills that loom
High in the distance fair,
Breezes that bear perfume
Sweet on the summer air.

Nothing to live for, pray?
Nothing worth while?
Look now where e'er you may,
Somewhere a smile;
Sunshine and morning dew,
Blue skies above us,
Hearts that are warm and true,
Someone to love us.

These are the joys of earth,
Wealth knows no more;
Laughter and song and mirth,
Flowers at your door,
Children to romp and play,
Skies that are blue;
Nothing to live for? Pray,
What 's ailing you?

DON'T WORRY, LITTLE GIRL

DON'T worry, little girl,
Don't you let one golden curl
Get awry.
Don't you ever let appear
E'en the symbol of a tear
In your eye.
For the world has need of girls
Who have sun-kissed golden curls,
And the world, with all its scheming,
Wants the light that's ever beaming
In a maiden's eyes today;
You were born for love and play.

Don't you worry, wife of mine,
Don't you ever show a sign
Of grim care;
Laugh and sing your way along,
All the grief and all the wrong
I can bear.
For along life's dusty miles
I have need of all your smiles,
I have need of all your laughter,
Let it ring from floor to rafter,
For, in all I say or do,
All my cheer must come from you.

Contentment ----

When e'er I'm sad, why then I'm glad
To think that I'm no sadder;
And when I'm glad, I'm a happy lad
To think none could be gladder.

CHARMS

SWEET is a rosebud, pink or red,
And sweet are the blooms of May,
And sweet is the fragrance about us shed
On many a summer day.
Oh, the world is full of such sweetness rare
To make our joys completer,
But there 's nothing so sweet on this earth, I swear,
But a baby's smile is sweeter.

Fair is the blue in the summer skies,
And fair is the summer sun,
And fair is the look in a sweetheart's eyes
When a man her heart has won.
The world is crowded with splendors fair
To gladden each burden-bearer,
But there 's nothing so fair on the earth, I swear,
But the charms of a babe are fairer.

Dear to us all are the friends we love,
And dear are the hopes we cling to;
And dear, indeed, are the memories of
The loved ones we used to sing to.
Oh, the world is crowded with treasures dear,
To our hearts, above all, they 're nearer;
But there 's nothing so dear you can mention here,
But the baby you love is dearer.

They Do n't ----

Life has its ups and downs,
Its fair and cloudy weather,
But this you 'll find, my friend,
They never come together.

DREAMING

JUST now I think
I 'd like to be
At the river's brink
Beneath a tree,
And stretched out flat
On the cooling grass,
Just gazing at
The clouds that pass
Like toy ships fair
In a sea of blue;
But I can't be there,
I have work to do.

Or I 'd like to be
In an orchard gay,
Where every tree
Is in bloom today;
Where the pink and white
Of the blossoms sweet
Blot out the fright
Of the city street,
Where there 's nothing to see
But what is true;
But that cannot be
For I 've work to do.

Oh, I'd like to steal
From my little den,
From the great unreal
And the haunts of men
To the joyous truth
Of the open air,
To the honest youth
That I left back there,

To the boy I was
    In the days of old;
But I can't because
    I 'm a slave to gold.

¶ Exercise is something that every man wants to get in any way possible so long as it does n't resemble work.

ENVY

OLD MAN, if I could have my wish
    As I take this cigar from you,
  It would n't be for wealth or fame,
For glory or an honored name;
    But it would be that I might, too,
Come down the street, my head awhirl,
And shout: "Friend, smoke, for it 's a girl!"

I envy no king, crown or throne,
    Nor Rockefeller all his wealth;
I envy no man's splendid home,
The leisure that he has to roam,
    I am content while I have health;
But in my heart I envy you,
Cigars I 'd like to pass out, too.

I 've lit your good cigar and now
    Are visions dancing in the smoke.
Time was my heart leaped with the thrill
Of joy as yours --- but now 'tis still,
    And I --- I sit and choke.
So, it 's a girl? Hooray! Hooroo!
But, pal o' mine, I envy you.

WHY I'M GLAD

I'M glad I have a wife at home
That's patient, kind and true;
I'm glad a little tot of three
At home waits for me, too;
I'm glad that I can see them both,
And hear them when they speak,
I'm glad that every night I feel
Their kisses on my cheek.

I'm glad that I am well and strong,
I'm glad that I can walk
And breathe the morning Springtime air,
I'm glad that I can talk;
I'm glad that I have friends who smile
A greeting when I come,
And I am glad that I can be
Each day a friend to some.

I'm glad that I have work to do,
And splendid books to read,
I'm glad that I can sleep at night,
I'm glad that I've a creed
Sustaining me in times of woe,
That soothes me when I grieve;
And I am glad that there's a God
In Whom I still believe.

I'm glad that I can laugh and sing,
I'm glad that I can play;
I'm even glad that I can eat
Three hearty meals a day.
I'm glad that life is as it is,
I'm glad my wants are small,
I'm glad for, oh, so many things,
I cannot name them all.

THE MAN OF HIS WORD

THE man of his word met a maid on the beach,
The fine art of swimming he offered to teach
If she 'd go with him in the water so blue.
She sighed and said: " Mister, if I go with you,
You must promise me faithfully here on the sands
That you won't splash the water at me with your hands;
You must honestly, solemnly vow and declare
That whatever you do you will not wet my hair."

So the man of his word, who had offered to teach
The gay little, sweet little maid on the beach,
Took an oath that he would n't splash water on her,
Or let any total immersion occur.
And the sweet little maid started gayly with him
To be taught how to float and be taught how to swim;
And the man of his word kept the vows that he swore,
He never once dampened the hair that she wore.

Alas, and alack! for the man of his word,
Next day came another who vowed and averred
That he would n't splash her or douse her, not he,
If she 'd only venture with him in the sea,
Which she did; but out there he forgot every oath,
For he doused her and splashed her, yes sir, he did both.
But did she rare up in her anger? Not she ---
Every morning you 'll find her with him in the sea,
While the man of his word sits alone on the beach,
And the bold, faithless wretch soon will marry the peach.

¶ If you want to know real appreciation, be kind to an old maid.

SUNDAY IN THE COUNTRY

SUNDAY in the country --- that's how we spent the day,
Drinking in the perfume of the fragrant breath of May;
Gazing at the splendors of the meadows and the hills,
Laughing with the babbling brooks and singing with the rills,
Dancing with the sunbeams and smiling with the skies,
And worshiping the Master with our hearts and minds and eyes.

Sunday in the country --- with an arch of blue above,
And the green trees whispering to us simple messages of love;
With the song birds singing anthems just as sacred and as sweet
And as stirring and uplifting as the church choir down the street;
In God's own great cathedral, where the poorest man may go,
And catch a glimpse of Heaven as he journeys here below.

Sunday in the country --- that's how we spent the day,
And we thanked God every minute for His precious gifts of May;
For the green trees waving o'er us as the shady lanes we strolled,
For the silver of the waters and the sunbeams' yellow gold,
For the fragrance of the lilacs and the apple trees in bloom,
For the glory of the sunshine and the blossoms' sweet perfume.

Sunday in the country --- till the shades of night came down,
When we turned our faces homeward and we journeyed back to town;
Back to all the ceaseless striving in the dreary haunts of men,
To the constant quest for money with its anguish once again,
But with faith in God above us, and serene contentment, too,
For our hearts were drenched with gladness as the fields are drenched with dew.

THE NOTION OF RASTUS

DERE never was a man on earth
So wonderful or clever,
Dat ever found a way t' live
On dis ole world forever.

Dere never was a man so rich,
Dat did n't have t' go
When ole man Death came after him
An' crooked his finger, so.

An' den dere never was a man
So great, when he was gone
But what dis good ole world of ours
Jes' kep' a-waggin' on.

An' since dis ole world never stops
When famous men depart,
I 've come t' de conclusion dat
We ain't so awful smart.

A HEART TO HEART TALK

THEY tell me that I 'm spoiling you,
The neighbors say that you should be
For all the awful things you do,
Laid face down over daddy's knee
And spanked and put to bed. That 's what
The neighbors say, but what say you?
You think you should be loved a lot?
Well, somehow daddy thinks so, too.

They tell me that it is n't right
For me always to take your part,
I 've heard it said you often fight,
And that you 'll break your mother's heart.
The neighbors say that you are bad
And should be whipped, but what say you?
You think you are too small a lad
To whip. Well, daddy thinks so, too.

What would you do if I were you,
And you were daddy, and they came
And told, as people always do,
My little deeds, and cried: "For shame"?
Would you put me across your knee
And spank me as you ought to do?
What 's that? You think you 'd try to be
Forgiving. Well, I think so, too.

¶ Tact consists of making people think that you think they 're as clever as they themselves think they are.

A wife will stand for the theory that old wine and old books are best, but do n't spring the old girl gag on her also.

A CREED

TO suffer with courage,
To smile though in pain,
To dream of the blossoms
When April brings rain;
To rise, if I can,
To the mountains aglow,
But still make the most
Of the valleys below.

To stretch out a hand
To a friend in distress,
To think more of truth
Than the emblem success;
To carry my burden
Straight up to my goal,
With love in my heart
And content in my soul.

To live in the world,
Not in sunshine alone,
A rounded experience
Here I would own;
To sip what is bitter
And taste of the sweet,
To come into victory
Knowing defeat.

To strive for the highest
But, though unattained,
To be glad of the distance
My efforts have gained;
To want to live on
For the friends who are nigh,
But still every day
To be ready to die.

DINNER - TIME

TUGGIN' at your bottle,
An' it 's O, you 're mighty sweet!
Just a bunch of dimples
From your top-knot to your feet,
Lying there an' gooin'
In the happiest sort o' way,
Like a rosebud peekin' at me
In the early hours of day;
Gloating over goodness
That you know an' sense an' clutch,
An' smilin' at your daddy,
Who loves you, O, so much!

Tuggin' at your bottle,
As you nestle in your crib,
With your daddy grinnin' at you
'Cause you 've dribbled on your bib,
An' you gurgle an' you chortle
Like a brook in early Spring;
An' you kick your pink feet gayly,
An' I think you 'd like to sing.
All you wanted was your dinner,
Daddy knew it too, you bet,
An' the moment that you got it
Then you ceased to fuss an' fret.

Tuggin' at your bottle,
Not a care, excepting when
You lose the rubber nipple,
But you find it soon again;
An' the gurglin' an' the gooin'
An' the chortlin' start anew,
An' the kickin' an' the squirmin'
Show the wondrous joy o' you.

But I 'll bet you 're not as happy
At your dinner, little tot,
As the weather-beaten daddy
Who is bendin' o'er your cot.

SINCE I HAVE DONE MY BEST

SINCE I have done my best, I do
Not fear the outcome; here I stand
Prepared for judgment when men view
The labor of my heart and hand.
If good, then happy I shall be,
If not, contented I 'll abide,
And though the prize is not for me,
My joy shall be in having tried.

Since I have done my best, there is
No cause for me to sit and sigh,
Although the laurel wreath I miss,
My eyes shall smiling be and dry;
No vain excuses shall I make
For failing, and no vain regret,
But bravely judgment I shall take,
And say: "A better man I 've met."

Since I have done my best, I 'll go
Whenever God shall summon me,
Contented, for right well I know
However poor my record be
That, having nothing to regret,
No shame that I would seek to hide,
The Master's praises I shall get
For honest effort when I tried.

DOUGHNUTS AND CIDER

LAST night I single handed fought a gang of murderers that came
To get my money or my life, and very nearly did the same;
I struggled with them on a cliff, and over it I toppled two,
I hit another one a biff that dazed him, but I was n't through,
As fast as one was overpowered another villain forced the fight,
Because four doughnuts I devoured and used a cider wash last night.

The horse that I was riding ran away with me at furious pace,
He tossed me up against a tree, I ploughed a furrow with my face!
A farmer's bull was grazing near, and he took up the battle then
And landed me upon my ear upon the farmer's cattle pen;
An aeroplane came whizzing by, I grabbed at it with all my might,
Because four doughnuts that you buy, with cider I washed down last night.

A strange and angry beast then came, a creature with a horrid grunt,
The way he used me was a shame, he galloped up and down my front;
He had the roughest kind of feet that ever I have gazed upon,

His breath was hardly fresh and sweet, of nostrils he had only one
But that belched fire and brimstone, too; his tusks were long and sharp and white ---
It 's awful what doughnuts will do when mixed with cider late at night!

A PRAYER

LORD, be my guide through the day
That 's beginning,
Teach me to strive and to play
Not for winning
Merely the glory that comes with success ---
Help me to fight for my soul's nobleness.

Lord, watch my hand, lest it fail
In the strife,
When temptations assail
And the pleasures of life
And its luxuries lure, give me courage to shun
The valleys of ease till my labor is done.

Lord, guide my feet, lest they lead
Me astray
From the worth of the deed
To the fame that I may
Less easily win; give me courage and might
Not to conquer, so much as to do what is right.

IF I WERE SANTA CLAUS

IF only I were Santa Claus I 'd travel east and west
To every hovel where there lies a little child at rest;
I 'd drive my reindeer over roofs they 'd never trod before,
I 'd seek the tenements where sleep the babies on the floor,
Where rags are stuffed in broken panes to keep the wind away,
And where a warm and cozy room is never known to-day;
For even there I know I 'd find hung up the stockings small
As signs that they expected me on Christmas Eve to call.

If only I were Santa Claus I 'd pass the mansions by
And seek the cold and cheerless homes where pale-faced youngsters lie;
And as they slept I 'd pause a while and bending low, I 'd kiss
The lips of every little tot --- not one of them I 'd miss;
And then I 'd fill their stockings full of toys and sugar plums,
And leave them sleighs and skates and dolls and Teddy bears and drums.
I would not pass a cottage by, but I would try to be
A Santa Claus to every tot who still has faith in me.

If only I were Santa Claus --- I 'd make the mothers glad,
The dear, hard-working mothers who at Christmas time are sad;

The kind and patient mothers who rock their babes to sleep,
And through the lonely hours of night sob bitterly and weep.
They see their precious little ones half clad and hungry, too,
Knowing the sorrow that must come to them when night is through;
To every mother's face I 'd bring the smiles once more, and we
Would spend a while together at her babies' Christmas tree.

¶ What a woman does n't know about her neighbors she soon finds out.

LIFE

A WEE bit of sorrow
And sadness and pain,
But sunshine tomorrow
And laughter again.

Some frowning, some sighing,
A wee bit of woe,
With tears quickly drying,
Thus Heavenward we go.

Some strife and resentment,
But far in the West
The Vale of Contentment,
The Haven of Rest.

THE TEMPTERS

EVERY gentle breeze that 's blowing is a tempter very knowing,
For it penetrates my armor in its weakest, thinnest spot;
Though I strive each day to shun it, I have never wholly done it,
For it whispers of enchantments that I know should be forgot.
Every moment it 's inviting me to go where fish are biting,
It is telling of the big ones that are lurking in the stream,
And the time I should be working, I am idling here and shirking,
From the duties of the office I am carried in a dream.

Every sunbeam that comes gayly into my grim office daily
Takes the courage from my bosom, makes of me a helpless thing;
It seems as though its mission is to rob me of ambition,
For I always pause to listen to the news it comes to bring.
Soft it mutters, "they are biting, it is great the way they 're fighting,
As I came from way off yonder I could see them in the bay,
Get your rod and reel and hurry, come away from all the worry!"
And once more I 'm dreaming, dreaming in the middle of the day.

Every breeze that passes by me, every sunbeam dancing nigh me,
Seem to mock me with their freedom and to tempt me from my task,
For they set me vainly wishing to go way off yonder fishing,
To stretch out beneath the willows on the velvet grass and bask.
Well they know my greatest weakness, my shortcomings and my meekness,
Well they know that if they whisper of a blue sky and a stream
Where the finny tribe is lurking, I shall promptly give up working,
And it seems their greatest joy is just to come and make me dream.

SUCCESS

I'D rather fail than have it said
I won by lying or deceit;
I want no laurel 'round my head
If winning it I have to cheat.

I 'd rather have the public jeer
And call me quitter, coward --- yes
I 'd rather stand to see them sneer
Than fraudulently gain success.

For winning is n't all of life,
Success is stamped upon the soul,
I 'd rather falter in the strife,
Than cunningly attain my goal.

MOTHER NATURE

GOOD, kindly Mother Nature plays
No favorites, but smiles for all
Who care to tread her pleasant ways
And listen to the song birds' call.
The tulips and the violets grow
For all the world to gaze upon;
With beauty are the hills aglow
Not for a few, but everyone.

Her grass grows green for rich and poor,
For proud and humble, high and low;
Beside the toiler's cottage door
Her morning glories sweetly grow.
In palace or in tenement
Her sunbeams just as gayly dance;
No special charm to one is sent,
No favored few possess her glance.

Her skies are blue for one and all,
Her flowers for every mortal bloom;
Her rains upon all creatures fall,
For all the world is her perfume.
The rich man gets no sweeter smile
Than does the ragged barefoot boy;
Yes, all who live and love the while,
May Mother Nature's charms enjoy.

Ah, what a lesson we may learn
From kindly Mother Nature's ways!
A smiling face we seldom turn
To strangers, when we meet their gaze.
A kindly word we seldom speak
Except unto a favored few,
And some return we often seek
For every kindly deed we do.

THE FIGHT WORTH WHILE

THE fight worth while on this good old earth
Is n't the fight for a hoard of gold!
It is n't the fight to increase your worth
In stocks and bonds and things to hold;
It is n't the fight for a higher place,
For a meed of power for a little while,
Or to finish first in the grinding race
And to bask in glory and pomp and style.

The fight worth while is the fight to be
Unfettered here by the cords of vice;
To set your soul from your body free,
To be unswerved by a yellow price;
To win the love of your fellowmen,
To be a man that they all respect,
To lose a fight but to fight again
With your shoulders square and your head erect.

This is the fight worth while today;
To have ideals and to cling to them,
To live your life in your own good way
In spite of the scoffers who may condemn;
To be willing to fail if the victory
Would lower your standard of what is right,
To be poor in purse, if you have to be,
But rich in spirit. Here is a fight!

To ask no favors from any man,
To conquer yourself, and to face the strife
With courage born of your own-made plan,
To do your best with your term of life;
To shirk no task that you find to do,
However bitter it seems to be!
And at last when the battle of earth is through
To be ready to die, is victory.

WHEN WE WERE KIDS

WHEN we wuz kids together, an' we did n't have a care,
In the lazy days of summer, when our feet wuz allus bare,
When a hat war n't necessary, an' a necktie in the way,
An' there war n't a blessed thing t' do but scamper off an' play;
Then th' sun meant somethin' to us, an' the blue skies overhead
Kinder stooped down in th' meadows where we children wuz, an' said:
" Trout are bitin' in th' mill stream, hurry up an' git yer pole,
Now 's th' time you should be hikin' 't' yer fav'rit fishin' hole."

When we wuz kids together, an' there war n't a thing t' fret,
'Cept comin' home t' mother with our hair suspicious wet,
Then th' sunbeams an' th' song birds used t' come t' us an' say:
" They are swimmin' in th' river, better git there right away,
As we passed 'em we could hear 'em laughin', splashin' down below."
Then we hurried t' th' river, jus' as fast as we could go,
For there war n't a thing t' keep us, like there is now we are men,
An' th' sunbeams an' th' song birds an' the skies meant somethin' then.

Now th' same sunbeams come callin', an' th' same song birds come near,

And the same blue skies bend o'er me and their messages I hear;
Every dancing sunbeam tells me that out yonder in the stream
Now the pickerel are biting, but I only sit and dream;
For I 've journeyed past my boyhood, I 'm a slave forevermore,
And I must not heed their whispers as I used to do of yore;
There are bills to meet and duties that I must not, dare not shirk,
Mr. Sunbeam, quit yer coaxin', it 's no use, I 've got t' work.

A SONG

COME fill your pipes and puff away,
Let 's sing our songs of gladness,
Put down your burdens of the day,
A fig for care and sadness!
A fig for care and sadness, Oh,
The night time 's ever jolly;
Good fellows, let your spirits flow,
Away with melancholly.

Come loose the bonds of honest mirth,
Let 's shake our sides with laughter,
'T is fellowship that rules the earth,
A fig for what comes after.
A fig for what comes after, Oh,
Tonight we 're free from sorrow,
Good fellows, let your spirits flow,
We may be dead tomorrow.

FOOD, CLOTHES AND DRINK

WHAT is food for, anyway?
Just to keep us through the day
Warm and strong and satisfy
Hunger, whether bread or pie,
Terrapin or chuck steak tough;
When a man has had enough,
What's it matter, anyway?
He can live and toil away.
Sigh you not for richer fare,
Bread and meat, with some to spare,
That is all the system needs,
That gives strength for noble deeds,
And the rich man, if you please,
Gets no more from luxuries.

What are clothes for, anyway?
Just to keep the wind at bay,
And to hide our nakedness.
Fine or homespun be your dress,
That is all that clothes can do,
They won't help nor hinder you;
Men in torn and tattered rags
Oft have borne their country's flags
Through the battle fire, and come
Back unto the sound of drum
Heroes, by the world extolled;
Be your garment new or old,
Still fight on with purpose true,
Finer dress can't conquer you.

What is drink for, anyway?
Just to quench your thirst by day;
Here is water, drink your fill,
It will leave you clear-eyed still;

It will moisten lips now parched,
Though ten thousand miles you 've marched,
Sparkling burgundy or wine,
Or the juice of any vine
Poured into a crystal cup
Will not better bear you up,
Will not better quench your thirst,
Better fit you for the worst;
Rich or poor, man cannot think
Of or buy a better drink.

KEEP TO THE RIGHT

KEEP to the right is the rule of the road,
Keep to the right as you travel along,
Often, for safety, your progress is slowed,
This is the rule for the weak or the strong.
Driving or walking this law all observe,
Now it 's adopted for aerial flight,
Get just as far as you can or deserve,
But always remember to keep to the right.

Make this the rule of your life every day,
Follow it out in all things that you do,
Guide of your tongue in all things that you say,
Guide to the goals that you seek and pursue.
Let it come first, though you win or you lose,
Conquer or fail in the thick of the fight,
This be the motto that daily you use,
This is sufficient, just "Keep to the Right."

A WONDERFUL WORLD

IT 'S a wonderful world when you sum it all up,
And we ought to be glad we are in it;
The fellow who drinks from old Misery's cup
Gets the goblet of joy the next minute.
In a wonderful way
In the course of a day
Strange changes occur as by magic,
There are solemn and sad things
And joyful and glad things,
And things that are comic and tragic.

It 's a wonderful world, full of wonderful things,
No two days alike in their passing;
Some new joy or sorrow the rising sun brings,
Some new charm the former outclassing.
And yesterday's glad
Are perhaps today's sad,
And yesterday's poor may be wealthy;
Oh, the changes are quick,
Even yesterday's sick
May today or tomorrow be healthy.

It 's a wonderful world, for we never can tell
What for us has the morrow in store;
Things happen as though by some magical spell
That never have happened before.
And nobody knows
Or can ever disclose
What the joy of the future may be;
But of one thing I 'm sure,
Despite all we endure
'T will be worth while to hang on and see.

THE LANES OF BOYHOOD

DOWN the lanes of boyhood, let me go once more,
Let me tread the paths of youth that I have trod before;
Let me wander once again where the skies are bright,
Freckled face and tanned of leg, roadways of delight,
Picking checkerberries as I laze along the way,
Hunting for the robin's nest --- dozing in the hay.

Down the lanes of boyhood, there are joys untold,
Hidden caves of precious things, stores of yellow gold;
Friends that only boyhood knows, birds and trees and flowers,
Nodding to the youngsters "Howdy do" in morning hours;
Skies that bend above them in the gentlest sort of way,
Fleecy clouds that seem to stop and watch them at their play.

Down the lanes of boyhood, hear their laughter ring!
See the tousled army marching straightway to a spring;
Flat upon the ground they fall, just to get a drink,
Here 's a thirst emporium where glasses never clink,
No glittering place of red and gold the passer-by to snare,
Yet, rich with Nature's coloring, a thousand times more fair.

Down the lanes of boyhood, where innocence abounds,
A medley gay of colors, a revelry of sounds;
Where hearts are never broken and wrong is never known,
Where sorrow never enters and no one weeps alone.
And yet we never can return when once we 've journeyed on,
Old age is ever wishing for the joys forever gone.

THE FAMILY PARTY

I SING the family party that once we used to know,
The old time family parties we gave so long ago,
When every near-relation and distant cousins, too,
The married ones with children, Aunt Mary and Aunt Sue,
The grandpas and the grandmas, yes, everyone of kin,
The nephews and the neices and some who married in,
Came trooping to the old home with laughter and with smile,
And had their fun together in the good old-fashioned style.

The games we played have vanished and gone beyond recall,
But I still can see the donkey that hung upon the wall,
And Uncle Ben blindfolded, his arm out like a flail,
Trying to find the proper place on which to pin the tail,
And I can hear the laughter that rose up like a roar,
When Uncle Ben had pinned it upon the parlor door;
And I can see the women folks sit on a crock and try
To pass a piece of linen thread right through a needle's eye.

The old time family parties, when Cousin Will would play
The square piano for us in a real heart-gripping way;
And Lil and Tom and Annie would take their turn and sing
Those songs which took your fancy and had the proper swing;
And when they tired of singing somebody would recite
A scene or two from Shakespeare and do the thing up right.

Then we 'd all sit down to supper, and I tell you, if
you please,
It was n't any dinky lunch you juggle on your knees.

But a real bang up collation, that 's what mother used
to say,
Of tongue and ham and cold roast beef --- it took her
'most a day
To prepare that supper for us --- there were jellies red
and fine,
And layer cakes and pound cakes and some cakes of
quaint design;
Oh, there 's nothing now can beat them though we 've
put on style and airs,
And adopted all the customs that obtain with millionaires,
We do n't have the fun we used to, nor the joy we
used to know,
At the old time family parties in the days of long ago.

The Man I Like ----

I like the man who stands right up
And takes his share of praise or blame,
And then, unchanged by loss or gain,
Treats all his neighbors just the same!

The man, who, if he liked you once,
Still likes you, though he 's gained success;
Who plays a man's part all the time,
And blames no friend for his distress.

WHAT A SICK WOMAN DOES

A CONVALESCIN' woman does the strangest sort
o' things,
An' it 's wonderful the courage that a little
new strength brings;
O, it 's never safe to leave her for an hour or two alone,
Or you 'll find th' doctor's good work has been quickly
overthrown.
There 's that wife o' mine, I reckon she 's a sample of
'em all;
She 's been mighty sick, I tell you, an' today can
scarcely crawl,
But I left her jes' this mornin' while I fought potater
bugs,
An' I got back home an' caught her in the back yard
shakin' rugs.

I ain't often cross with Nellie, an' I let her have her
way,
But it made me mad as thunder when I got back home
that day
An' found her doin' labor that 'd tax a big man's
strength,
An' I guess I lost my temper, for I scolded her at length;
'Til I seen her tear drops fallin' an' she said: "I could-
n't stand
T' see those rugs so dirty, so I took 'em all in hand,
An' it ain't hurt me nuther, see I 'm gettin' strong
again --- "
An' I said: "Doggone it! Can't ye leave sich work as
that fer men?"

Once I had her in a hospittle fer weeks an' weeks an'
weeks,

An' she wasted most t' nothin', an' th' roses left her cheeks;
An' one night I feared I 'd lose her; 't was the turnin' point, I guess,
Coz th' next day I remember that th' doctor said: "Success!"
Well, I brought her home an' told her that for two months she must stay
A-sitttn' in her rocker an' jes' watch th' kids at play;
An' th' first week she was patient, but I mind the way I swore
On th' day when I discovered 'at she 'd scrubbed th' kitchen floor.

O, you can't keep wimmin quiet an' they ain't a bit like men,
They 're hungerin' every minute jes' t' get t' work again;
An' you 've got t' watch 'em allus, when you know they 're weak an' ill,
Coz th' minute that yer back is turned they 'll labor fit t' kill.
Th' house ain't cleaned t' suit 'em an' they seem t' fret an' fume
'Less they 're busy doin' somethin' with a mop or else a broom;
An' it ain't no use t' scold 'em an' it ain't no use t' swear,
Coz th' next time they will do it jes' the minute you ain't there.

¶ It 's all right to leave your grouch at home, but it 's much better never to take it there.

A WOMAN'S WAYS

IT 'S human for a woman
To enjoy a little cry;
Though a man will grin and bear 'em
And pass little troubles by,
A woman seeks a pillow
And her face she buries in it,
Starts the bitter tears to running,
And she 's better in a minute.

It 's human for a woman
To expect a lot of fussing,
Though a man will greet his fellow
Without once his topknot mussing;
A woman greets her sister
Disarranging gown and hair,
Kissing, hugging, squeezing, gurgling,
With enthusiasm rare.

It 's human for a woman
Not to know just what she wants,
That 's the reason she goes shopping
And the down-town stores she haunts;
Though a man knows just exactly
What he wants and goes and gets it,
A woman spends time looking,
And she never once regrets it.

It 's human for a woman
To enjoy a lettuce sandwich,
Though a man wants steak and onions
And a cup of " Mocha and " rich;
She must have her lady fingers,
Ices, tea and macaroons,
And she gets her fun in toying
With the solid silver spoons.

Man must grin and bear his troubles,
    Lovely woman always cries,
And the man who 'd seek to stop her
    Does a thing that 's most unwise;
Let her weep and kiss in greeting,
    Shop and feed on dainty fare ---
These are human for a woman,
    They 're her meat and drink and air.

¶ There is a call for back numbers now and then, but do n't be one for that reason.

GOSSIP

A FELLOW can't help hearing
    Hateful things about another,
But a fellow can be careful
    Not to tell them to his brother.

Sit and listen, if you want to,
    When the spiteful things are said,
But do n't pass on the scandal,
    Keep a still tongue in your head.

Spread no little tale of evil,
    Whether right or whether wrong,
You may harken unto gossip,
    But do n't send the tale along.

THE LITTLE OLD-FASHIONED CHURCH

THE little old-fashioned church, with the pews
that were straight-backed and plain,
Where the sunbeams to worship came in through
the windows that bore not a stain,
And the choir was composed of the good folks who
toiled week-days in meadow and lane;

The little old-fashioned church that stood on the brow
of the hill,
With its plain, wooden cross on the peak, an emblem
of love and good will,
Of the Christ who has died for us all --- in fancy I gaze
at it still.

I wish I could go there again and list to the preacher
who told
Of the wonderful joys that await us when God calls us
into His fold,
Who pictured a Heaven unto us as a city with pave-
ments of gold.

The little old-fashioned church with never a towering
spire,
With never a sign of great wealth, and the people who
sang in the choir
Giving their music for love of the cause and not for
the sake of their hire.

Perhaps I am wrong or old-fashioned or queer, but the
little, gray church on the hill,
Where only God's mercy and love were e'er preached,
the want in my life seemed to fill,
And I do n't get the comfort I seek from the church of
today with its frill.

A WOMAN'S LOVE

THERE are times a woman's love
Fer a man stands out, I guess,
More 'n usual, like as when
Sickness comes or else distress;
But I reckon that it shines
Brighter than a taller dip
When a man is goin' away
An' she comes t' pack his grip.

'Pears t' me she seems t' think
More about his comforts then;
Puts in slippers, jes' as though
They were worn by traveling men;
Fusses round an' round th' room,
Hopin', maybe, that she 'll see
Somethin' that perhaps he 'll need ---
Jes' as thoughtful as can be.

Packs in heavy underwear,
Fearin' that it may get cold;
It is most remarkable
What a common grip will hold
When a woman fills it up ---
Things fer sunshine an' fer rain,
Pills fer every kind of ills,
Liniment fer every pain.

Seen her pack that grip o' mine
Hundred times, I guess, an' more;
Heard her sigh while doin' it,
Kneelin' on th' bedroom floor;
An' I never went away
On the shortest kind o' trip
Without feelin' that her heart
Had been packed inside my grip.

THE OLD-FASHIONED COOKS

POETS have sung of the old-fashioned glories
The old-fashioned pictures that hung on the wall,
The old-fashioned people, the old-fashioned stories,
The old-fashioned fashions they love to recall;
The squeaky armchair that our grandmothers sat in,
The old-fashioned shelves with their old-fashioned books,
Immortalized have been in Saxon or Latin,
But I sing my song to the old-fashioned cooks.

O come, all ye gods! and give grace to my ballad,
Today I would sing as I ne'er sang before;
I 'm heartsick of dining on lettuce and salad,
And canned goods warmed over delight me no more.
I wish I could go once again to a dinner
That had n't been planned out of style sheets or books ---
They may be all right for a sweet young beginner,
But they were not needed by old-fashioned cooks.

How well I remember the table cloth spotless,
The dishes that shone like the cheek of a child,
The jellies and relishes, O, there were not less
Than eight or nine kinds on the festive board piled.
There were no little dabs served to make you ungrateful,
They took it for granted, I guess, from your looks
That hunger was yours, and they gave you a plateful
Of viands most toothsome, those old-fashioned cooks!

You came to their tables to eat, not to chatter,
And heaped were the plates that they passed up to you;

In richest of gravies the meat in the platter
    Was swimming, and side dishes never were few.
They fed us with plenty, not starved us with fashion,
    They gave us enough and they cared not for looks,
And just now with me it is almost a passion ---
    I yearn for a dinner by old-fashioned cooks.

¶ A good husband never talks back to his wife; a good wife never gives him occasion to.

AT THE SUMMER COTTAGE

FATHER 'S in the woodshed,
    Cleaning forty fish;
Mother 's in the kitchen,
    Washing every dish;
Sister 's upstairs making
    Every bed we own;
The company is on the porch
    With the graphophone.

Father does the rowing,
    Brother does the chores,
Mother does the baking,
    Sister sweeps the floors;
Everybody 's working,
    Here at Idlenook,
Except the company --- and that
    Sits down and reads a book.

MOTHER'S PARTY DRESS

"SOME day," says Ma, "I 'm goin' t' get
A party dress all trimmed with jet,
An' hire a seamstress in, an' she
Is goin' t' fit it right on me;
An' then, when I 'm invited out
T' teas an' socials hereabout,
I 'll put it on an' look as fine
As all th' women friends of mine."
An' Pa looked up: "I sold a cow,"
Says he, "go down an' get it now."
An' Ma replied: "I guess I 'll wait,
We 've other needs that 's just as great.
The children need some clothes t' wear,
An' there are shoes we must repair;
It ain't important now t' get
A dress fer me, at least not yet;
I really can't afford it."

Ma 's talked about that dress fer years,
How she 'd have appliqued revers,
The kind o' trimmin' she would pick,
How 't would be made t' fit her slick,
The kind o' black silk she would choose,
The pattern she would like t' use;
An' I can mind the time when Pa
Give twenty dollars right t' Ma,
An' said: "Now that 's enough, I guess,
Go buy yourself that party dress."
An' Ma would take th' bills an' smile,
An' say: "I guess I 'll wait awhile;
Aunt Kitty 's poorly now with chills,
She needs a doctor and some pills,
I 'll buy some things fer her, I guess;

An' anyhow, about that dress,
I really can't afford it."

An' so it 's been a-goin' on,
Her dress fer other things has gone;
Some one in need or some one sick
Has always touched her t' th' quick;
Or else, about th' time 'at she
Could get th' dress, she 'd always see
The children needin' somethin' new,
An' she would go an' get it, too.
An' when we frowned at her, she 'd smile
An' say: "The dress can wait awhile."
Although her mind is set on laces,
Her heart goes out t' other places;
An' somehow, too, her money goes
In ways that only mother knows.
While there are things her children lack
She won't put money on her back;
An' that is why she has n't got
A party dress of silk, an' not
Because she can't afford it.

Be Cheerful ----

The world is bright and sunny ---
If you have n't any money,
What 's the difference?
Let me ask you anyhow.
Let the other fellow hurry,
Let the other fellow worry,
You won't know a thing about it
In a hundred years from now.

THE REASON FOR WORK

SOME struggle hard for worldly fame,
Some toil to have an honored name,
And some have great ambition.
A few there are who strive that they
May save the heathen far away,
Which is a noble mission.
Still others work for riches vast
To have enough when youth is past
For charitable giving;
Yet millions of us work by day,
And this our object is alway:
To make a decent living.

This is the secret of our toil,
For this we burn the midnight oil,
For this the rhymester sings.
'T is want that spurs us on, not fame,
'T is hunger, not a world-wide name ---
The need of worldly things.
Though fame may come in after years,
And in his ears may ring the cheers
And plaudits of the crowd,
'T is not for them man toils today,
But that his wife and babies may
Be decently endowed.

That he may have enough to wear,
Enough to eat, enough to spare
To give to those in need,
Is, after all, man's purpose true,
'T is all the good man hopes to do;
For more than that is greed.
The greatest things are done by those

Who face privation and its woes
And seek to climb above them;
The men who rise to fame, you 'll find,
Take thought of first and keep in mind
The needs of those who love them.

MOTHER

OH, mother, why do you spin and weave,
And why do you toil today?
And what do you sew in this fading light?
Come, put all your work away.
But the mother smiled, and she said: "I toil
For the babe that is sleeping there,
Tomorrow his father takes him forth,
And he must have a suit to wear."

Oh, mother, your eyes are heavy now,
Come, it is time to sleep;
Weary your fingers are, I 'm sure,
Why do you toiling keep?
But the mother smiled, and she said: "I toil
For the love of my children three,
Tomorrow their father takes them forth,
And proud of them I must be."

Ah, mother, toiling by day and night---
Only God understands
The patient love of a mother's heart,
The strength of a mother's hands.
And I think tonight as I watch you sew,
Still toiling the way you do,
As you are proud of your children three,
So God must be proud of you.

THE CHRISTMAS SPIRIT

IT 'S HO for the holly and laughter and kisses,
It 's ho for the mistletoe bough in the hall!
Was ever a season so jolly as this is?
No, this is the jolliest one of them all.
The season of loving and giving and dancing,
The season of mirth and of hearts that are true,
The season of eyes most bewitching, entrancing ---
It 's ho, Merry Christmas! A welcome to you.

With loved ones about us to laugh at our follies,
The patter of feet in the hallways above,
A ring at the door --- now deserted are dollies ---
All rush to greet callers and shower them with love.
What turbulent romping! Was ever such shouting
So dear to the heart and so sweet to the ear?
Away with all fretting, repining and doubting,
Ye, ho, for the Christmas so brim full of cheer.

Away with you, Trouble! Our armor of gladness
You can't penetrate with your arrows of fear;
Away with you, Sorrow! Away with you, Sadness!
Our walls are defended this morning by Cheer.
A fig for your frowning, Old Gloom, and your grouching,
No pessimist enters our castle today;
And should to our doorway a Kill-Joy come slouching,
We 've sentries of Cheer who will drive him away.

¶ The average woman finds it easy to economize when buying Christmas presents for her husband's relations.

THE AFTER-DINNER SMOKE

THROUGH the smoke clouds that I blow
I can see the Long Ago
And the merry lanes of boyhood
That I gayly used to tread;
See the crows upon the wing,
Hear the thrushes sweetly sing,
And once more I 'm stretched out dreaming
With the green grass for a bed.

As I slowly puff away,
I 'm a boy once more at play,
I am angling for the catfish
Or I 'm swimming with my chums;
Now I chaw green apples, too,
Underneath God's stretch of blue,
With not a thought of trouble
Or the pain that after comes.

As the blue smoke slowly curls,
Once again I see the girls
In their little gingham dresses
And their faces berry-brown;
Then one little maid I see
Who was all in all to me
In the days before I journeyed
From the old home to the town.

Now she comes into the room
Where I 'm dreaming in the gloom,
And she says the air is frightful,
And she starts to gasp and choke;
But, of course, she does n't know
How the days of Long Ago
Come back to me each evening
In my after-dinner smoke.

SOMETIMES I git to thinkin' o' the days o' youth, an' then
There comes a-troopin' through my mind th' wimmin folk an' men
I used ter know in Pixley, an' I sit with 'em awhile,
A-livin' all th' fun we knew before we put on style;
A-dancin' all th' dances, th' lancers an' q'drilles,
A-goin' to th' huskin' bees an' picnics on th' hills,
An' I quite ferget I 'm livin' on a crowded city street,
Where I don't know a quarter of th' people that I meet.

I settle in my arm chair, an' I light my meerschaum pipe,
An' then I 'm back in Pixley with the apples red an' ripe.
I 'm makin' eyes at Agnes, which is wrong I must allow,
Coz she was married long ago an' has four babies now.
An' I 'm pokin' fun at Lydy, who was in for any joke,
But she has married wealthy --- still out yonder in th' smoke
She is still the laughin' lassie, free from all the haughty airs
That wimmin folk think needful when they marry millionaires.

Then I steal a kiss from Nellie, an' I hear her say "No, no!"
Th' way she did a thousand times, but never meant it, though.
An' again from church we 're comin', an' th' hour is gettin' late
An' we stand awhile a-gabbin', she a-swingin' on th' gate,

A-tellin' of her uncles an' her aunts, an' how they were,
While all that I was wantin' was to stay an' talk of her.
An' again I 'm gettin' ready jes' to ask her to be mine,
An' again she ups an' leaves me, sayin' "Ed, it 's after
nine."

O, I tell you what! It 's funny, when I think about it all,
An' I kinder get to broodin' an' th' old days I recall
When there warn't no automobiles, warn't no problem
plays an' such,
When th' only fault with young folks was they loved
t' play too much;
When there warn't no style about us, one warn't richer
than another,
When we did n't think of money, never snubbed a poor-
er brother;
An' to see 'em now with riches, an' ashamed to even
say
That they ever lived in Pixley--- Why, my soul is there
today!

¶ What is only honest pride in ourselves
is unbearable conceit in others.

True ----

The shoemaker sticks to his last and he 's right;
By divorce, though, we wouldn't be cursed,
If everyone else in this great world of ours
Would be willing to stick to his first.

GARDENING

GARDENING is hardening
In every way you view it;
It makes a fellow hustle,
And it strengthens every muscle;
It knots up many a tendon
So that no one can undo it;
It starts his back to aching,
And the man who 's busy raking
Out the cobble stones and paving bricks
Is very apt to swear;
O, gardening is hardening,
It keeps wives busy pardoning
The hubbies who are spilling
Heated language on the air.

Gardening is maddening
And gladdening and saddening,
It 's tiring and inspiring,
And at times a dreadful bore;
It keeps a fellow coping
With potato bugs, and hoping
That his radishes will equal
Those you purchase at the store.
It is full of grim surprises,
Disappointments it comprises.
It has all the elements of work
And pleasure's roundelay;
For one morn you find your roses
Shriveled up. The next discloses
That the lettuce should be edible
About the end of May.

Gardening is vexing,
There 's no doubt it is perplexing,

There are many things about it
We don't understand and can't;
Why the lettuce we have tended
Carefully, when all is ended,
Should resemble in its toughness
Leaves from wifie's rubber plant;
Why the radishes we nourished
In a cool place, where they flourished,
As we followed the directions
Of the seed man to a jot,
Should appear to us inviting
And delude us into biting,
Just to find that salamanders
Never could be quite so hot.

Still we keep on ever hoeing,
Planting garden truck and sowing
Many vegetables, knowing
What the future has in store;
And we till the soil with vigor,
Every man must be digger,
Though he cuts a sorry figure
When the harvest days are o'er.

What We Can Be ----

We cannot all be men of fame,
We cannot all be men of wealth,
We cannot all be known by name,
We cannot all have perfect health,
We cannot all be men of power,
We cannot all be of one mind;
But we can all be, every hour,
Hopeful, cheerful men, and kind.

MONEY

HE 'D made a fortune out of stocks, he could n't
count his worth;
He 'd hoarded up a store of gold, a section
of the earth;
But still he sighed alone and talked of all the world's
distress,
And mentioned to his dearest friends: "Gold won't
buy happiness."

Within his mansion big and warm he often cried aloud:
"There is no joy in being rich, no charm in being
proud;"
But still the morning saw him frowning, cross and
very glum,
Unless he added to his store another goodly sum.

"Ah, me," he often used to say, "indeed it 's very true,
There are so many things in life that money cannot do;
It cannot purchase peace of mind nor make a con-
science clear;
It cannot, when the soul is sad, make sorrow disappear."

"You do not know what gold can do," a friend of his
replied,
"You little guess its purchase power, because you
have n't tried;
Go, take your money out today, and see what it will
buy;
Go, feed the hungry little child and note his twinkling
eye.

"Go, help the brother in distress --- an old man starts
today
Across the hills to die within the poorhouse far away;

Give him a little of the gold you 've hoarded to excess,
Then tell me if you can that money won't buy happiness.

"The money that is hoarded up will buy no peace of
mind,
But money rightly used will bring much comfort you
will find;
And if for others but a part of what you have is spent,
You 'll find the happiness you crave, and you will live
content."

THE MAN I'M FOR

I'M for the happy man every time,
The man who smiles as he goes his way,
Whether he 's up or whether he 's down,
I 'm for the man with a grin, I say.
I 'm for the man who can bear his woes
With never a grumbling word or frown,
Who, smiling, gathers the rue or rose ---
There is the man that you can't keep down.

I 'm for the cheerful man, heart and soul!
His is the hand that I like to grasp;
Who tunes his voice in a merry key,
Not files it down to a bitter rasp.
I 'm for the man who can take the cards
Just as they 're dealt by the hand of fate,
And, good or bad, play an honest game
With a lifted chin and a smile that 's great.

THE DREAMS OF YOUTH

THE dreams of youth are fairest,
The dreams of youth are rarest;
The dreams of youth are brighter
Than the dreams we 'll know again.
Hope is the fairy weaver
For youth, a firm believer,
And great the things we 'll master
In the days when we are men.

There 's neither pain nor sorrow
In the great and grand tomorrow
For the boy who lies a-dreaming
Underneath the apple tree.
There 's neither hate nor malice
In the shining, golden chalice
The painter of the future holds
For every boy to see.

For his eyes are turned to gladness
And he sees no tear of sadness
In the visions of the future
That his soul is drinking in.
In the days to come he 'll journey
With a brave heart to life's tourney,
And he dreams about the prizes
That in future years he 'll win.

But the dreams of age are dreary,
For the soul is, O, so weary,
And the mind goes back in sadness
To the deeds we might have done;
And, too late, we sit repining,
Soon our sun will cease its shining,
Deep regret now paints the picture
Of the prize we might have won.

Ah, the future is the brightest
And its troubles are the lightest,
For the past is filled with anguish
And with disappointments, too.
Age has trod the paths of sorrow,
He has known each glad tomorrow,
But youth is ever dreaming
Of the things he 's going to do.

¶ It is n't sweet music when you hear a man blowing his own horn.

THE SPENDTHRIFT

HE died a poor man, so they say,
Few were the dollars stored away
By him while he lived, and yet
His memory I 'll not forget.
A spendthrift! True, but not for self
He scattered thus his hard-earned pelf;
Not that he might in splendor roam,
But for the ones he loved at home.

A spendthrift! That he was for those
Who, weeping, watched his eyelids close;
For them he toiled, for them he spent
His pittance and was well content.
The best in life to them he gave,
Denied them nothing just to save;
For those at home his coin he blew,
I would the world more spendthrifts knew.

ON STATION FAREWELLS

IN parting from a dear old friend for months, perhaps, or years,
There 's bound to be some bitter sobs, an' generally tears,
An' as a rule, the lovin' ones will gather round about
The station, softly cryin' while the train is pullin' out;
Oh, it 's so hard to say good-bye, an' kiss each tender cheek,
Coz there 's a lump in every throat, an' no one dares to speak.
Good-bye is always hard to say to friends you know are true,
But ten times harder when the train that waits for them 's in view.

When comes the time for me to go upon a little trip,
I always wait until the last before I pack my grip;
An' always try to hide the fact that I am goin' away,
An' do my best to keep the folks in cheerful mood an' gay.
A railroad station 's mighty glum when friends are goin' out,
It sorter shakes a fellow's nerve an' fills his heart with doubt;
An' so I'd rather say good-bye at home the times we part,
An' then sneak on the train alone --- it 's easier on the heart.

There 's something 'bout a train that leaves a depot with your friends,
That fills your soul with grievin' an' a thrill of sorrow sends
All over those who watch it, till it disappears from sight,

An' the bravest can't help cryin' when it fades into the night.
I love to have them meet me when I 'm comin' home once more,
But when I 'm goin' from them, then I kiss them at the door
An' wave my hand in partin', as I hurry down the street,
An' then sneak on the train alone, an' sink into my seat.

Outgoing trains are sad ones --- incoming ones are gay,
It is n't hard to tell the folks who 're goin' far away;
In stations little groups are seen, an' O, so oft, I note
A mother tryin' hard to down the lump that 's in her throat;
It seems she 's tied her heart-strings to the train that 's waiting there,
An' the tug that comes at partin' is far more than she can bear;
An' I 've come to this conclusion, that whene'er I have to roam,
I 'll board the train unnoticed, with my "good-byes" said at home.

Failures ----

Some men must a-wooing go
And fail to win the girl,
Some must search through oyster shells
And fail to find the pearl;
Men must toil and men must fail,
Not every plan goes right,
And some men must a-fishing go
And fail to get a bite.

CHRISTMAS EVE

BACK UP Old Age and Wrinkled Face,
Come, Selfish Grown-Up, quit the place,
You Pessimist, depart!
Now, Gloomy Gus and Doleful Frown,
There is no room for you in town,
Nor Bitter Ache and Smart;
Childhood tonight is King of Earth,
Make room for Laughter and for Mirth!

Step down a moment, Out-for-Fame,
Hard-headed business man, the same,
And You, who won't believe;
Move on now, Lust-for-Gold, make way
For Innocence and Youth and Play,
For this is Christmas Eve;
Bowed-down-by-Care, make room, make room,
Let little ones dispel the gloom.

Soured-on-the-World, you 've had your fling,
You 've been a failure as a King,
Your reign at last is done.
And you, grim prophet of Despair,
Who view no thing on earth as fair,
Make way tonight for Fun;
Your citadels are overthrown,
Tonight Youth comes unto the throne.

Envy and Hate and Haughty Pride,
'T is time for you to turn aside,
Let Love and Childhood pass;
The night of nights has come once more,
E'en Sorrow journeys from the door,
Come, little boy and lass,
The world is yours, ascend the throne,
Your subjects we, and yours alone.

MAN'S EXPERIENCE

A SCRAMBLE for gold,
And a scurry for place,
A brief pause for loving,
A kiss, an embrace,
A ring; then the altar,
A vow to be true,
Then back to the turmoil
To scramble for two.

For man 's the provider,
And ever he strives
To care for his loved ones
And brighten their lives.
A year or so passes,
Still toiling is he,
"A boy!" says the doctor,
"Now scramble for three."

For this is the common
Experience of men,
A small raise in salary
Comes now and then.
But ever we hurry
And scramble by day,
For the fam'ly increases
As fast as our pay.

Bravery ----

The brave man journeys straight ahead;
The coward goes
Along his way in constant dread
He 'll meet a friend in need, ahead,
Or one he owes.

A BABY'S LOVE

A BABY is the best to love,
She always smiles when you draw near,
Though ugly you may be of face,
No handsomer may interfere
And win her heart away from you,
Despite your faults she 's always true;
And though you be unknown to fame,
A baby's love remains the same.

A baby's eyes are always bright,
A baby's lips are always red,
And, O, a baby's voice is sweet,
Though not a word she 's ever said.
A baby loves you for yourself,
She 's not entranced by sordid pelf;
Though other loves may leave a smart,
A baby never breaks your heart.

It matters not though you be poor
And friendless in the outside world,
The moment that you cross the door
That baby in your arms is curled.
Though all the world may jibe and jeer,
A baby smiles when you draw near;
Through joy or sorrow, weal or woe,
With you, a babe is glad to go.

Ah, lucky man, indeed, is he
Who has a babe at home to love;
All that men now are striving for,
He owns a treasure far above.
Though fate may rob him of his gold
And bare him in the winter's cold,
And drag him down to deep despair,
His baby still will count him fair.

INDEPENDENCE DAY

WHAT does it all mean anyway,
Noise of cannon and boom of gun,
Deafening, colorful fire display
Starting in with the rising sun?
Ah, it means that this land of ours,
Fringed with mountains and decked with flowers,
Warm with sunshine and wet with dew,
Is dear to the hearts of her people true.

Every whizzing rocket that seeks the sky
And bursts in beauty, the world above
Proclaims aloud, as it journeys high,
A nation's pride and a nation's love;
It seems to speak of her wonders here,
Her mines so rich and her skies so clear,
Her harvests grand and her waving pines,
Her fields of green and her creeping vines.

Oh, a glorious day is this day we keep!
For under the noise and the powder scent
Is a strain of love that is wide and deep,
A touch of a nation's sentiment.
Love of country the cannon speaks,
Love of freedom the rocket shrieks,
Love of the flag that waves above,
This is the meaning --- a nation's love.

A Fourth of July Wish ----

This is the day when we are great,
And sally forth to celebrate;
When night comes on, God grant that we
Have ears to hear and eyes to see.

MY CREED

THIS is my creed: To be simple and kind,
To rise every morn with a song in my heart;
To the faults in my brothers to ever be blind,
And bravely to journey, content with the part
I am playing in life; to be gentle and true,
To suffer in silence what crosses may come;
Unstintingly praising the good men I view,
When speech would be bitter to ever be dumb.

A kiss for my loved ones each morning and night,
A glad word of greeting for all whom I meet;
To keep my home happy and cheerful and bright,
A haven of rest and a spot that is sweet.
To live every day as though it were my last,
To strive to complete every task that 's begun,
To go to my couch when the daylight is passed,
Content that I 'm leaving no kind deed undone.

This is my creed: Not to wince nor to falter,
But bravely to battle alone with grim fate;
No duty to dodge, and no principle alter,
To compromise never with wrong, to be great.
To succeed if I can with my crest still unspotted,
But gladly to fail if to win would mean shame;
To live all unknown with my honor unblotted,
Than hailed by the throng with a stain on my name.

¶ What with keeping the refrigerator full and the pail underneath it empty, man has his troubles.

The prettier the vase, the more burned matches you are apt to find in it.

IS THERE A SANTA CLAUS?

"IS there a Santa Claus?" she asked,
"Come, daddy, tell me true;
I heard today the good old saint
Is really, truly, you;
That no one down our chimney comes
To little girls and boys,
That you and mama really buy
My dollies and my toys."

I held her on my knee and gazed
Into her searching eyes;
Somehow, I 've felt this time would come,
This question would arise;
And yet, I pondered to myself,
What shall I say or do,
And then I answered: "Yes, there is
A Santa Claus for you.

"He comes to you on Christmas Eve,
But let me tell you this:
He 's with you when you hug your dad,
And when his cheek you kiss;
He 's with you when you say your prayers
To God, who reigns above;
Sometimes he has another name,
We grown-ups call him Love.

"You keep your faith in Santa Claus
When others bid you doubt,
You still retain your faith in him,
Let not belief die out;
And, what you heard today is wrong"---
I felt the tear drops start ---
"Yes, yes, there is a Santa Claus,
He lives in daddy's heart."

MY WORD!

YOU can tyke h'it from me, 'e 's as cool as a cucumber,
Never goes balmy h'or loses 'is 'ead,
Nothing h'at all h'ever robs 'im of slumber;
Once when I told 'im 'is rich h'aunt was dead,
'E looked h'at me blandly,
H'and stryngely h'and grandly,
H'and stroked 'is moustache as though 'e 'ad n't 'eard;
Flicked a speck h'off 'is coat,
H'and then cleared h'out 'is throat,
H'and put on 'is topper, remarking: "My word!"

Cool h'as an h'oyster along h'in December ---
Once h'I was riding with 'im h'in a tryne,
The detyles h'I cannot h'exactly remember,
But something went wrong with th' bally h'old line.
There cyme h'a great crash,
H'and a 'orrible smash;
H'I shouted h'at once: "Something h'orful 's h'occurred!"
'E 'eard women crying,
H'and looked h'at the dying,
H'and cooly survying the scene, said: "My word!"

Larst week 'is h'old 'omestead was burned down to h'ashes,
H'and while h'it was burning they notified 'im;
The firemen were shouting h'and myking mad dashes
To rescue 'is wife, but their charnces were slim;
At larst, through the smoke
There h'appeared h'a bryve bloke
With 'is wife h'in 'is arms, h'an' they slowly descended;

Then did 'e go dotty
With h'ectasy? Not 'e ---
'E merely remarked: "O, my word, that h'is splendid!"

¶ When a woman does n't know which way to turn she 's usually getting off a street car.

LOVE

TRUTH went forth on a search one day
For the source of love that he might say
He had found its depth and its breadth for aye.

He met a miser, bent and old,
And his mission to him he promptly told;
"Love," said the miser, "is yellow gold."

He sought a maiden, young and fair,
With orange blossoms in her hair,
Who whispered, "My love is waiting there."

To a struggling youth at last Truth came,
As he toiled and studied and spoke his name;
"Love," said the youth, "is a thing called fame."

"Love!" mocked a man with features sour,
Before whom others were made to cower,
"Love! yes, love is worldly power."

A pale, weak woman Truth chanced to see,
Rocking a baby on her knee;
"Only a mother knows love," said she.

UP AND DOWN THE LANES OF LOVE

UP and down the lanes of love,
With the bright blue skies above,
And the grass beneath our feet,
O, so green and O, so sweet!
There we wandered boy and girl,
Sun-kissed was each golden curl;
Hand in hand we used to stray,
Hide-and-seek we used to play;
Just a pair of kids were we,
Laughing, loving, trouble free.

Up and down the lanes of love
With the same blue skies above,
Next we wandered, bride and groom,
With the roses all in bloom;
Arm in arm we strolled along,
Life was then a merry song,
Laughing, dancing as we went,
Lovers, cheerful and content;
No one else, we thought, could be
Quite so happy as were we.

Up and down the lanes of love,
Dark and gray the skies above;
Hushed the song-birds' merry tune,
Withered every rose of June.
Grief was ours to bear that day,
All our smiles had passed away,
Sorrow we must bear together,
Love must have its rainy weather,
Keeping still our faith in God,
As the lanes of love we trod.

Up and down the lanes of love,
Still the skies are bright above.
Feeble now we go our way,
Time has turned our hair to gray;
Rain and sunshine, joy and woe,
Both of us have come to know.
All of life's experience
Has been given us to sense;
Still our hearts keep perfect tune
As they did in days of June.

THE BENEFIT OF TROUBLE

IF LIFE were rosy and skies were blue
And never a cloud appeared,
If every heart that you loved proved true,
And never a friendship seared;
If there were no troubles to fret your soul,
You never would struggle to gain your goal.

It 's trouble that makes you and proves your worth,
It 's trouble that spurs you to better things.
It is n't the man with the joys of earth
Who courage and strength to his duty brings;
But the man who bends 'neath a burden great
Is the man who wins in the fight with fate.

It 's something to work for, a debt to pay,
A place to gain that a young man needs;
The difficulties that line the way
Are really the mothers of splendid deeds.
The man with something he hopes to do
Is the man who toils with a purpose true.

ENDURANCE

YOU never hear a woman boast
Of her endurance, yet I vow
The tiniest mite o' a woman has
More courage than a man, somehow.
Lor' bless me, when I hear a man
A-braggin' how he kep' right on
A pluggin', fightin' to'ards his goal,
With all his hope of winnin' gone,
A-puffin' out his chest with pride,
It makes me smile, becoz I know
If he 'd a woman's cross t' bear,
'At he 'd a give up long ago.

It 'pears t' me 'at woman is
Jes' equal parts o' nerve an' grit;
There is no task too great fer her,
She does n't know such word as quit.
I 've seen her when I knew her strength
Was failin' faster every day,
Still workin' on without complaint,
Findin', in some mysterious way,
The power t' overcome her aches,
An' all the weariness she knows.
Endurance! Nothin' ever yet
Has equaled what a woman shows!

An' when her back was like t' break,
An' man would plumb discouraged be,
I 've heard a little woman say:
"The children need so much from me
I 've got t' work," an' then she 'd start
Washin' an mendin' little clo'es;
An' then sit up till late at night
Darnin' the holes in little hose.

It mattered not how sick she wuz,
No task o' hers she ever shirked,
When man would quit an' go t' bed
That little woman bravely worked.

An' so it allus makes me smile
T' hear a man git up an' say
'T is wonderful what he endured,
An' how he worked from day t' day;
An' then t' tell in boastin' style
The hardships that he underwent,
Explainin' how he kep' his nerve
Although his strength was nearly spent.
For when it comes t' downright grit,
An' bearin' troubles great an' small,
An' winnin' spite of everything,
A little woman beats 'em all.

SONGS OF GLOOM

IF the song I have to sing
Is a dreary, gloomy thing,
I would rather silent be;
If I cannot sing of cheer,
I will never let you hear
Any song of dole from me.

Let no dirge escape my lips,
Rather song that gayly trips
Than a slow and mournful tone;
Let me sing a song of pleasure,
In a romping sort of measure,
But my woe I 'll bear alone.

CHUMS

HUSBAND and wife for fourteen years!
And just like children now,
As fond of one another as
The day they took their vow.
Where he goes she goes, hand in hand,
And thus their record sums,
Through all those years of joy and strife
They really have been chums.

Husband and wife. No, more than that,
For husbands oft are known,
In search of pleasure now and then,
To journey off alone;
And wives have clubs and other things
That interest them more
Than business plans their husbands make,
When honeymooning 's o'er.

Not so with them --- through weal or woe,
Through sunshine and through rain,
Together they have journeyed on;
She cheered when all seemed vain.
His greatest joys have always been
The ones that she could share,
We knew that when we saw the one,
The other must be there.

If I could change the marriage rite
That binds a pair for life,
'T would be to drop that stilted phrase,
"You 're husband, now, and wife."
For just one little word, I think,
The knot far more becomes;
I 'd like to hear the parson say:
"Beloved, now you 're chums."

OUR LITTLE NEEDS

A LITTLE more of loving, a little less of pain,
A little more of sunshine, a little less of rain;
A little more of friendship, a little less of strife--
These are what we 're wanting to make the perfect life.

A little more of laughter and fewer, fewer sighs,
A little more of twinkling, than sorrow in our eyes;
A little more forbearance, a little less of hate,
A little more of patience, less quarreling with Fate.

A little more of kindness, a little less severe,
A little more of sweetness, a little less austere,
A little more of honor and less of business greed,
See, brother, see how little it is we really need!

A little more of silence and less of hasty speech,
A little more of practice and less desire to preach;
A little more of smiling, with fewer drooping chins,
A little more of virtues, with fewer petty sins.

A little more of praising, a little less of blame,
More thought for all our loved ones and less for future
fame;
A little more of doing than talking of the deed,
See, brother, see how little it is we really need.

Similiar ----

A warship and a woman's hat
Are just alike, I state,
They 're big and ugly, cost a heap,
And soon get out date.

THE GLORIES OF THE PRESENT

WHAT of the glories after death,
When this frail form gives up its breath?
Why do we strive to understand
The Future when the Now 's at hand?
What matters it to you and me
That o'er some dark mysterious sea
Whereon we all must sail some day,
Awaits a port where we must stay?

It is enough for me to know
A brighter place there is to go;
I ask not when will come my time,
Whether the road is hard to climb,
What glories there await for me;
I would not solve Death's mystery
And still live on --- I am content
To live the life that God has sent.

Now is the problem that I strive
To solve, while I am yet alive;
What am I here for, what to do?
Am I unto my purpose true?
Do I live, every day a man,
Helping and cheering where I can?
Am I employing every hour
For deeds of good, my gift of power?

This is what I prefer to know,
Not when or whither I must go;
No thought of Future lines my brow,
Mine is the problem of the Now.

My hopes are not on after-death,
But on today while I have breath;
If I have done my best while here,
I 'll face hereafter without fear.

AFTER A PROPOSAL

IS IT so sudden? Then did you believe, dear,
Those evenings I called at your flat
And lovingly, longingly gazed in your eyes,
That I merely had come for a chat?
Did it strike you the times that I lingered till twelve
And hated to leave you alone,
I was doing that merely to fill up my time,
Because I 'd no home of my own?

So sudden, you say? Yet for years I have stood
On your doorstep each evening at eight.
Did you think I had come for a chat with your ma,
Or a word with your maiden aunt, Kate?
Did you think, when I sighed as I fondled your hand,
'T was dyspepsia that troubled me then?
Or that the cigars I bestowed on your dad
Were smokes I would give to all men?

O, the tickets for shows I have purchased for you,
The automobiles I have hired!
The lockets and bracelets and purses and things,
All gifts that I knew you desired,
That I tenderly laid at your feet, as a shrine,
Though each cost me a half a week's pay!
I thought that my actions betrayed my design,
And yet, " It 's so sudden," you say.

BACK TO SCHOOL

it ain' the ringing of the bell
which calls me back to skule once more;
it ain't that i must lurn to spell
that makes my hart so orful soar:
it ain't that fracktions i must lurn
nor jografy that makes me blew,
it 's just becoz today i yurn
to do the things i did n't doo.

ring out, wild bell! ime on mi way
to skule again, and summer 's done ---
it dussent seem more than a day
since i began to have mi fun.
i would n't mind this cuming back,
it ain't the skule ime kicking on,
it 's just becoz i missed a stack
of fun, and now the summer 's gone.

i planned to bild a coogie in
our yard, where all the kids could meat;
the roof was going to be of tin,
and we 'd have carpet for our feet;
and i was going to organize
a brave and daring pirut crew
and we 'd take rich men bi surprize ---
but gee! how fast the summer 's flue.

and that 's the skule bell ringing now,
vacashun 's slipped away from me;
what i acomplisshed anyhow
is something more than i can see;
i 've had some fun, of course, but then,
it really seams to beet the dutch
how very little i did when
i planned to do so very much.

Ah, little boy, you do not know
The lesson that you teach us all;
You with unwilling feet now go
To school at the approach of Fall.
We grown-ups soon will hear a bell,
Announcing that our course is run,
Far more than death we fear to tell
The good deeds that we might have done.

LILLIAN'S READING

AIRY, fairy Lillian,
What a naughty thing to do,
By noon had read a Laura
Libbey paper novel through.

By four o'clock another
Tale of love and passion trite
She had devoured, and on the third
Was well along by night.

But in the kitchen, Lillian's
Mother toiled with dish and spoon,
Endeavoring to work, and get
A lunch for dad at noon.

She washed the dishes, scrubbed the floors
And made each bed by four,
And even ironed every waist
That lovely Lillian wore.

Thus every Laura Libbey book
That lovely Lillian reads,
Is built on mushy love affairs
And mother's noble deeds.

THE NEW YEAR'S CALLER

COME, open your door, there 's a friend waiting near
Who is eager to wish you a Happy New Year;
He rings at the bell and he 's ready to shout:
"The New Year is in and the old year is out;
And long may you prosper and long may you smile,
May happiness dwell with you all the while."

Come, run to the door! There 's a friend waiting there,
Go bid him to enter, and draw up his chair;
Come, fill up his wine glass and pass him the cake,
For fewer and fewer are calls that friends make;
Come, shout in reply to his message of cheer:
"Long life to you, friend, and a Happy New Year!"

"A Happy New Year and a wealth of success,
May love and prosperity never grow less;
May each year that follows be happier, too,
May Time and Grim Sorrow deal gently with you."
Come, run to your door! There 's a friend waiting there,
Invite him to enter and draw up a chair.

Come, open your heart! There 's a friend waiting near
Who is eager to share in your sorrow and cheer;
He longs for your friendship, and fain would he win
The way to your heart. Will you not let him in?
He knocks at the door. Would you send him away
Or greet him with love and implore him to stay?

¶ And there are some men who will do their best and even their best friends.

LITTLE GIRL

WHAT'S a book, compared to you,
Little girl?
There's no story half so true,
Little girl;
Come now, clamber on my knee,
You bring more of love to me
Than my whole great library,
Little girl.

Yes, I came in here to read,
Little girl;
But a book I do not need,
Little girl;
All the printed line could tell,
You impart with magic spell,
Love and laughter with you dwell,
Little girl.

I would be a churlish dad,
Little girl,
If for you no time I had,
Little girl;
Clamber on my knee tonight,
You can give me more delight
Than the books that great men write,
Little girl.

You're a volume full of love,
Little girl,
Published up in Heaven above,
Little girl;
Every word of yours rings true,
Sweet the little deeds you do,
I shall never tire of you,
Little girl.

FOR OTHERS --- AND HIS WIFE

HE took off his hat to the woman next door,
But he would n't do that for his wife;
He picked up the handkerchief dropped on the floor,
But he would n't do that for his wife;
He ran for a chair when a fair maiden stood,
Did everything that a gentleman should,
When leaving he helped her get into her hood,
But he would n't do that for his wife.

He offered his arm to the fair Mrs. Brown,
But he would n't do that for his wife;
He gallantly carried her parcels from town,
But he would n't do that for his wife;
He helped her alight from the trolley car then,
Did n't stand on the platform to smoke with the men,
But sat down beside her. I 'll say it again
That he would n't do that for his wife.

If it 's proper these little attentions to pay,
Then he ought to pay them to his wife;
No man is polite, let me venture to say,
If he is n't polite to his wife.
Fair woman deserves all our courtesies --- true,
And enough for her no man is able to do,
But the man who 's a gentleman right through and through,
Is a gentleman first to his wife.

¶ Do n't worry about other people's troubles unless you really mean to do something to relieve them.

YOU AND YOUR BOY

WHOM is your boy going to for advice?
Tough Johnny Jones at the end of the street,
Rough Billy Green or untaught Jimmy Price?
Who is now guiding his innocent feet?
Who takes him walking or swimming today,
You, or the stranger just over the way?

Whom is your boy leaning on for a friend?
Whom does he tell all his wee troubles to?
Say, now, with whom does your little one spend
Most of his time; with a stranger or you?
Whose hand is leading him where he should go?
Answer now, Busy Man, tell if you know.

Who is the pal that he opens his heart to,
You, or some stranger you never have seen?
Whom does your boy all his secrets impart to?
Maybe to some one whose mind is unclean.
If it isn't to you that he comes, he 's in danger.
What do you know of the worth of the stranger?

Oh, be a boy with a boy that is yours;
Play with him, stay with him, show him the way;
Walk with him, talk with him, take him out doors;
Be his best friend, as you ought to, today.
Take him down town so the youngster may see
The right sort of man that you want him to be.

Don't be too busy to hear what he 's telling;
Don't send him off when he comes to your knee;
This sort of father disaster is spelling ---
He 's hungry for you, and his pal you should be.
Spend all the time that you can with the lad,
He 'll be a good boy if you 'll be a good dad.

THE CONTENTED MAN

I'VE had a heap of fun and I've had a heap of sorrow,
I've had a heap of pleasure and I've had a heap of pain,
But I'm treading just as gayly, just as bravely toward tomorrow,
And I'm looking for the sunshine, but I'm ready for the rain.
Always hoping for the best,
For the peace and perfect rest,
Always hoping for the sunshine and the roses dripping dew;
But should gloom and sadness come,
They will find me never glum,
I will greet old grim misfortune with a cheery howdy-do.

I've had a heap of laughing and I've had a heap of sighing,
I've had a heap of sadness and I've had a heap of mirth;
And I've come to the conclusion that in spite of all our trying,
We are bound to meet some sorrow as we journey on the earth.
For the best I'm always praying,
But life is n't always playing,
And whatever is my fortune, be it good or dismal quite,
I will try to take it bravely,
And to view my duty gravely,
Still believing that what happens is inevitably right.

I've had a heap of winning and I've had a heap of failing,

I 've had my share of praises and I 've had my share of blame,
And I've come to the conclusion that life's sea on which we 're sailing
Is made up very justly of proportions of the same.
For the calm and pleasant weather
I am thankful altogether,
And I'm hopeful, ever hopeful, that no more storm-tossed I 'll be;
But should storm clouds quickly lower,
I will neither shrink nor cower,
But I 'll face the gale serenely and I 'll try to ride the sea.

O, I 've known a lot of people, and I 've heard of many others,
But I never knew or heard of one who had n't tasted woe;
All the fathers here and brothers here, the sisters and the mothers,
Must meet with disappointments and with sorrows as they go.
Not a one that Fate has missed,
Or a sunbeam left unkissed,
Each has tasted pain and pleasure, each has suffered good and wrong;
So, while hoping for the best,
I am ready for the test,
I will face whate'er is sent me, and I 'll sing my way along.

¶ The difference between an irritable man and a flannel undershirt is that you can walk away from the irritable man.

UNDER A TREE

UNDER a tree where the breezes blow,
There is the spot that it's good to go
With the children bronzed by the
Summer sun,
Bubbling with laughter and wholesome fun;
And I gather them round --- all the happy clan,
And forget for a while I'm a grizzled old man.

Marjorie, Florence, and fair Lucille,
Freddy and Denny --- and then we steal
An hour or two from the clock of life,
The quest of gold and the constant strife,
The clamor and noise of a city day
For the peace and joy of a bit of play.

Pirate stories for boys we tell,
For there is the place to tell them well;
With treasure islands we build in sand,
And we mark the spot where the pirates land,
And even the place where the gold was hid
By that master of pirates, old Captain Kidd.

Then we leave the pirates and run away
To the wonderful glens where the fairies play;
And under the tree where the breezes are
We summon the fairies with crown and star,
And I tell of the wonderful things they do
When the sun is up and the skies are blue.

And the far off world may call and call,
But I never hear through my little wall
Of innocent youngsters that hem me in.
I finish one tale and a new begin;
And there we sit underneath the tree
Till mother calls all of us in for tea.

THE BANK ROLL

(With Apologies)

HOW dear to my heart is the bank roll departed,
The five-spots and tens in the strong rubber band,
The yellow boys, too, that were mine when I started,
And oft I caressed with a fatherly hand.
The wide, bulging bank roll that set my eyes popping,
The bank roll I had when we struck the hotel;
The bank roll she touched when she journeyed out shopping,
The bank roll now vanished that served us so well.
The wide, bulging bank roll, the rubber bound bank roll,
The bank roll now vanished that served us so well.

How sweet from the green, crinkled wad 't was to peel one,
And flash it about for the strangers to see;
How splendid to know that the wad was a real one,
And all it was made of belonged unto me.
Now the tear of regret in my sad eyes is welling,
Once again I am making the poverty yell;
And I sigh, as I sit in my poor, humble dwelling,
For the bank roll now vanished that served us so well,
The wide, bulging bank roll, the Michigan bank roll,
The rubber bound bank roll that served us so well.

¶ Making hay while the sun shines is all right, but hats off to the man who keeps on trying to make hay when the sun is n't shining.

The pay envelope is the best proof of a man's ability.

HOME

IT takes a heap o' livin' in a house t' make it home,
A heap o' sun and shadder, an' you sometimes have t' roam
Afore you really 'preciate the things yer lef' behind,
An' hunger fer 'em somehow, with 'em allus on yer mind.
It don't make any differunce how rich yer get t' be,
How much yer chairs an' tables cost, how great yer luxury;
It ain't home t' yer, though it be the palace of a king,
Until somehow yer soul is sort o' wrapped round everything.

Home ain't a place that gold can buy or get up in a minute,
Afore it's home there's got t' be a heap o' livin' in it;
Within th' walls there's got t' be some babies born, an' then
Right there you've got t' bring 'em up t' women good, an' men;
An' gradjerly as time goes on, yer find yer wouldn't part
With anything they ever used—they've grown into yer heart;
The old high chairs, the playthings, too, the little shoes they wore
Yer hoard; an' if yer could ye'd try t' keep th' thumb marks on th' door.

Ye've got t' weep t' make it home, ye've got t' sit an' sigh
An' watch beside a loved one's bed, an' know that Death is nigh;

An' in the stillness o' the night t' see Death's angel
come,
An' close the eyes o' her that smiled an' leave her
sweet voice dumb.
Fer these are scenes that grip the heart, an' when yer
tears are dried,
Yer find the home is dearer than it was an' sanctified;
An' tuggin' allus at yer are the pleasant memories
Of her that was and is no more --- ye can't escape
from these.

Ye 've got t' sing an' dance fer years, ye 've got t' romp
an' play,
An' learn t' love th' things ye have by usin' 'em each
day;
Even the roses 'round the porch must blossom year by
year
Afore they 'come a part o' you, suggestin' some one
dear
Who used t' love 'em long ago, and trained 'em jes' t'
run
The way they do, so 's they would get the early mornin' sun;
Ye 've got t' love each brick and stone from cellar up
t' dome,
It takes a heap o' livin' in a house t' make it home.

Roses and Gasoline ----

"A rose by any other name would smell as sweet,"
Cried Romeo once, and truth he spoke I own;
And we should smell the autos down the street
Though gasoline were labeled French cologne.

REUNITED

THE hours were long with you away,
Although I thought I could forget;
I banished you and cursed the day
That we had ever met.

I frowned upon you, and I vowed
That nevermore your charms I 'd seek;
I sought new pleasures with the crowd,
But I am weak.

Temptress I called you, and I swore
No longer your demands I 'd serve;
Freedom I 'd own forevermore,
But lost my nerve.

And absent, all my love returned,
Not for one moment was I free,
For you I nightly, daily yearned;
Your slave I 'd be.

No charm in anything I found,
No lustre in the skies of blue,
I merely moped my way around,
And sighed for you.

I must be made of fragile clay,
Unsuited for the hero type,
For back to you I come today,
Old briar pipe.

¶ If your boss has a poor opinion of you, you can make up your mind that your boss is about 90 per cent right.

THE CARD CLUB'S FIRST MEETING

THE battles for the pickle dish once more are under way,
The Uno Pedro Club is first and foremost in the fray.
It started off auspiciously, without a sign of frown,
Good Mrs. Green put all at ease by kissing Mrs. Brown.

Then Mrs. Johnson graciously kissed Mrs. Jackson's lips,
And Mrs. Watson followed suit by kissing Mrs. Phipps;
Then all formality was dropped, and everyone grew cheery,
When Mrs. Rich, the president, called Mrs. Bilkins "dearie."

I can't describe the sweetness and the tenderness displayed,
No one remarked that Mrs. Gray was once a lady's maid;
With arms around each other's waists they sat and planned things out,
And everyone was loving and no one wore a pout.

I listened to her story, and a gentle smile I wore,
I 'd heard of women kissing and of loving ones before;
And I wondered as I heard her rave about the lovely meeting,
Just which of them will be the first to be accused of cheating.

¶ It never occurs to a young girl, but it 's often the truth nevertheless, that the money the young man spends on her when they go out together was borrowed from his mother just before he left home.

GIVE ME A SINGLE DAY

GIVE me a single day, I ask no more
From dawn to dusk, ah, that is time enough
To reach the goal that I am striving for;
There is no need of further putting off
The little deeds of kindness I may do,
The little words of kindness I may say;
I need no distant morrow to be true,
Give me a single day.

Give me a single day to live my life,
For that is time enough for smiles and tears;
I can as bravely bear my share of strife
As though I were to live a thousand years.
I can be brave and patient and resigned,
Helpful and cheerful as I go my way;
I need no distant morrow to be kind,
Give me a single day.

Give me a single day, 't is all I ask,
And let me fill each minute with my best;
I can complete my little daily task,
And find contentment in my hour of rest.
I may not journey many, many miles,
But I can view the roses where I stray,
I need no distant morrow for my smiles,
Give me a single day.

I do not ask to be allowed to live
Another year or twenty, so that I
When richer to the poor may proudly give,
Neglecting now the chance that is close by.
I would not spend today in seeking gold,
Saving tomorrow for the kindly deed;

To prove that I am cheerful, helpful, bold,
Only a day I need.

Let me but live a rounded life today,
My virtues all in action as I stroll;
For further time I would not ask or pray,
Upon the future I 'd not risk my soul,
For in the time I have much I can do,
Fearless, yet gentle in my simple way;
I need no distant morrow to be true,
Give me a single day.

THE LIMITATIONS OF GREATNESS

NO MAN really knows enough
To be hateful to his brother,
None is rich enough to cuff
And be cruel to another;
None so clever that he can
Justly wrong his fellow man.

No one is so strong that he
Has the right to curb the weak,
None so great that properly
He can trample down the meek;
There is nothing in success
That excuses selfishness.

Climb unto the topmost hights,
Win yourself an honored name,
But respect another's rights,
Raise the weak and help the lame;
Strength of muscle or of mind
Gives no right to be unkind.

THE OLD DAYS

WHEN I was but a little tad I used to hear my
dear old dad
Tell friends about the good old days forever gone from him;
My dear old kindly gran'dad, too, explained the merry
joys he knew,
When he was in his twenties, and could dance and
run and swim;
The burden of their song always was this --- the good
old bygone days,
The days of thirty years ago, when all the world
was gay,
And folks were always merry then, and men were bigger, better men,
And fun was funnier by far than what it is today.

When I was young I could n't see, how such a state of
things could be,
For I was having fun myself, and plenty of it, too;
And not so long ago I told --- a sign that I am getting
old ---
About the good old days that once upon a time I
knew;
I found that like my dear old dad, I thought about the
joys I had,
And I was sure that times had changed and fun had
ceased to be;
I often heaved a bitter sigh, and wished and wished
for days gone by;
The old days were the happy days, or so they seemed
to me.

But looking back in history, unto the time we call B. C.

I find that dads and gran'dads then were living in
the past;
Old Julius Caesar, who was slain, once sat and sighed
and wished in vain
Because the joys that once he knew were not allowed
to last.
Before Noah built his famous ark, I 'll bet some ancient
patriarch
Beneath his vine tree sat and said the days of fun
were gone,
That times were not as once they were, that joys had
vanished from the air,
And fun and mirth and merriment somehow had
wandered on.

And so today I 've ceased to talk and ceased to let my
thinker walk
Away back where the old days are --- I 've ceased to
call them best;
I 've got the notion that today is just as happy, just as
gay
As any yesterday of mine, and just as full of zest.
Tomorrow will be just as bright, and just as full of
rare delight
For those who follow me as were the golden days
of yore;
And when I hear some croaker say, there 's no such
thing as fun today,
I get his derby, coat and cane and show him to the
door.

¶ A woman is always happiest when she is telling what she would do if she were a man.

The better the cook the sooner she quits to get married.

COMRADESHIP

OF ALL the ships that sail life's sea,
The Comradeship 's the one for me;
In weather fair or weather foul,
A pleasant breeze or gales that howl,
An ocean smooth or troubled sea,
The Comradeship rides merrily.
Her masts are staunch, her sails are white,
Her compass true, and day or night
She keeps her course, and in the end
Comes back to port with every friend.

The Comradeship is manned by men
Who teach the sad to smile again;
True-hearted souls who 've quaffed the glass
Of bitterness and seen it pass;
Who know the meaning of distress,
The heartache and the weariness
That those who journey here below
Sooner or later come to know;
And on the deck they stand and smile
And bid us fare with them a while.

They bid us make a pleasant trip
Upon the gallant Comradeship;
With them they bid us pace her deck,
A friendly arm about each neck,
And back to hearts with aching sore
They bring the balm of peace once more;
And from the troubled sea of strife
They bring us to the joy of life,
Restoring hope and faith again
To weary and despairing men.

Of all the ships that sail life's sea
The Comradeship 's the one for me.

Her cabin rings with laughter true,
Above her skies seem ever blue,
And by the sunlight of a smile
She steers for "Happy Afterwhile;"
The port of Consolation, too,
She touches ere her journey 's through;
And this the song her master sings,
"Our destination 's Better Things."

A NEW YEAR'S WISH

MAY all your little cares depart
By which your heart is troubled;
May perfect peace supplant the smart,
And all your joys be doubled.
May every wish you have come true,
And every sky above be blue.

May every foe become your friend,
And every wrong be righted;
And may your paths that wind and bend
With sunshine all be lighted.
May love and laughter walk with you,
With ne'er a tear the whole year through.

Good health, good friends, good luck, I pray
That you will always know,
With lips to kiss at close of day,
And eyes with love aglow.
Where 'er you go, a hand clasp true,
This is my New Year's wish for you.

AUTUMN

THE leaves are falling one by one,
The Summer days are past and gone,
The nights are cool and damp;
The little children think it strange
At tea-time, for they note the change,
We have to light the lamp;
To roost the chickens earlier go,
And everything has ceased to grow.

The pumpkins now are big and round,
And turning yellow on the ground,
The leaves are drifting down;
The farm seems bigger than before,
'T is stripped of all its wondrous store;
Only the russets brown
Still linger on the trees, and they
Will soon be picked and packed away.

The cellar 's stored with rare delights
To while away the winter nights;
The squeaking cider mill
Is gushing forth its nectar rare,
A drink that all the gods call fair;
And O, the world is still;
A hush has settled over all,
The Summer 's gone and it is Fall.

Footwear ----

" What will you have to eat? " I said,
And she replied:
" Shoe string potatoes, tongue --- and Ed,
Some sole well fried."

THE KINDERGARTEN MISS

THE little kindergarten miss,
Source of all my joy and bliss,
Every evening in the window
Waits and watches just for me;
Waits and watches for her daddy,
And I see her waving paddie
As I hurry, hurry homeward
In the twilight joyfully.
Then when I have snatched a kiss
That sweet kindergarten miss
Cries: "Now, daddy, come and see it,
Come and see what I have made!
Here 's a picture frame for you,
Made of paper, white and blue!"
And I look upon her labors
Half exulting, half afraid.

Oh, you kindergarten miss,
You have made far more than this,
You have made my heart beat faster
Than it ever beat before;
As your little work you 're showing,
You have set my eyes to glowing,
And my tears will start up flowing
In another minute more.
Though this picture frame of blue
Does n't now mean much to you,
Little kindergarten lassie,
It 's a treasure rare to me!
And those fingers that have made it,
On my heart have also laid it,
And your face is in the center
For the god of love to see.

THE DON'T - BELIEVERS

THE new - fangled churches that don't believe things
Are n't the churches that satisfy me;
I 'm firm in my notion that angels wear wings,
An' Heaven is a place we shall see,
I 'm an old-fashioned man, full of old-fashioned ways,
An' these up-to-date doubtings seem odd;
What they don't believe folks talk about nowadays,
But I 'm still believing in God.

Some don't believe this, an' some don't believe that,
Some don't believe Heaven is a place;
The don't believe sermons they 're preaching are flat,
For of old-fashioned faith there 's no trace.
They 've torn up the Bible an' proved it 's not so,
They doubt man was made from a clod,
What they don't believe seems to be all that they know,
But I 'm still believing in God.

There is n't much left of religion today,
The thinkers have busily swept
Most all of the faiths that we once had away,
An' few of us know what they 've kept.
It 's "don't believe this" an' "don't believe that,"
An' blinded they 'd leave us to plod;
An' old-fashioned man hardly knows where he 's at,
But I 'm still believing in God.

What men don't believe does n't interest me,
I 'd far rather learn what they do;
I believe in the green of the grass an' the tree,
I believe in the sunshine an' dew;
I believe in the love that makes living worth while,
I believe we shall rise from the sod

To a mansion in Heaven where our dear ones shall smile,
An' I 'm still believing in God.

FOUND OUT

"NEVER again," said Mrs. Green, as she swayed in her rocking chair,
"Never again will I think one house big enough for two to share;
Never again will I go away with another family,
I 've had a month of that game this year, and once is enough for me.

"I fried the fish and I stood all day in a kitchen stifling hot,
While Mrs. Burroughs, arrayed in pink, sat out in a shady spot;
And we were to share in the work, you know, but little the work she did;
Whenever there was any work to do she hurried away and hid.

"Her children --- impudent little brats --- were always abusing mine,
They were always yelling for something, too! In a week I was sick of their whine;
Oh, she 's all very nice in town, I know, when her hair has the proper friz,
But you 've only to live with that woman a week to know what she really is."

HIS FIRST LONG TROUSERS

SAY, young fellow, just a minute,
They 're your first long trousers, eh?
And your little gray knee breeches
Are forever put away.
And your blouses and your stockings,
And your little caps are gone,
For the shirts and cuffs of manhood,
And you 've got a derby on!

Yes --- you look well in them, sonny,
Why, I can't believe my eyes!
For it does n't seem a year ago
Since you were just this size,
And a little, pink-cheeked youngster;
Why, you toddled more than ran
Every night to meet your daddy,
And today you are a man!

Oh, I don't know how to tell you,
But I want to, yes, I do,
That your mother and your daddy
Both are mighty proud of you;
And we 're going to miss the baby
That from us today has gone,
But that baby we 'll remember
Though he has long trousers on.

We 're banking on you, sonny,
We 'll help you all we can,
But it 's up to you, remember,
Now to prove you are a man;
You can make us mighty happy,
You can make us mighty sad,
Just remember it 's not manly
To do things you know are bad.

I 'm not going to preach a sermon;
Mother 's put your blouse away
And your breeches, and I saw her
Crying over them today;
And I thought perhaps I 'd give you
Just a thought to dwell upon,
Please remember, you 're her baby,
Though you 've got long trousers on.

A WISH

IF GOD should come and say to me:
" What is your dearest wish to be?
What high position do you crave
This side of Heaven and the grave? "
I 'd merely say: " Pray let me be
The father of a family."

I would not ask to rule the land,
To live within a palace grand,
I would not ask for wealth or fame,
To write in history my name;
I 'd merely say: " Pray let me be
The father of a family."

Oh, little girl upon my knee,
Your daddy I would rather be
Than any king or prince or earl;
And so, you see, my little girl,
Just why your daddy 's always glad,
His fondest, dearest wish he 's had.

WHEN PA GETS BACK

I'M allus glad when my Pa gets back
From the shu-shu cars and the railroad track,
Or a big boat ride, which he often does,
Oh, I 'm orful glad when he 's back becoz
Jes' as soon as he 's kissed my ma an' me
He laffs, an' says: "Come along an' see
The wonderful things in my old black grip,
The things I got on my little trip."

Nen he puts his grip on a parlor chair,
An' he says to me: "Now stand right there
An' we 'll jes' see what is inside o' this,
But first we 'll all have another kiss."
Nen he opens his grip, an' it 's jes' crammed tight
With toys an' things. Oh, I wish you might
Be there some day when my Pa gets back
To see the things in his old grip sack.

There 's allus a doll for his little girl,
Which is me --- a doll with a yellow curl:
An' the very last time that he went away
I really could n't begin to say
All the wonderful things that he brought to me
Coz I 'd been good, as I said I 'd be;
I 'm sure that I could n't tell them all,
But one was a new pink parasol.

An' he brought me some books an' some candy, too,
An' anuvver dolly all dressed in blue,
An' a broom jes' made for a girl like me,
An' the nicest hair ribbons ever you see,
An' a spade an' a rake to dig in sand,
An' some dishes my Ma says are Heavyland;
I cry when my Pa goes away, but when
He gets back home I am glad again.

THE AVERAGE MAN

MINE is a song of the average man
Who has been on earth since the world began!
You 'll find him kind and you 'll find him true,
You 'll find him cheerful and happy, too.
He 's never proud and he 's never mean,
He walks the earth with a conscience clean,
The squarest fellow that God could plan
On earth today is the average man.

He loves his wife and he loves his home,
He is n't the fellow who likes to roam;
He keeps his love for his fellow man
And bears his burden as best he can;
He 's a gentle neighbor, a faithful friend,
And will fight for him to the bitter end;
The decentest fellow that God could plan
On earth today is the average man.

The average man does n't cheat or lie
Or wrong his brothers. He does n't try
To climb to glory and gain the crown
By pulling a weaker brother down.
He 's always found on the side of right,
His creed is always a spotless white;
And oft as the wrongs of the world I scan,
I thank the Lord for the average man.

The Peevish Man ----

When he has suffered honest woe,
I do not mind the man who grieves,
But I hate him who stubs his toe
And straightway gets a case of "peeves."

SEPTEMBER

SEPTEMBER with her brushes dipped in dazzling red and gold
Now comes to paint the valleys and the hills;
And we forget completely that the year is getting old
As we gaze upon the color that she spills.
For all that we remember
Are the glories of September,
The bloom upon the peaches and the gold upon the grain,
The apples red with blushes
From September's crimson brushes,
The glory of the hill tops and the splendor of the plain.

September --- magic artist --- comes again to paint the trees,
Comes again to crown with beauty Mother Earth;
And she 'll touch with gold or crimson every humble plant she sees,
Without questioning its merit or its worth.
And the eye that looks to see
On the frailest little tree
Will behold a touch of glory where September it caressed,
And the poorest little bloom
That is soon to meet its doom
Will be nodding in the sunshine with the proudest richly dressed.

And September makes me think as I watch her splashing paints
Over every living thing underneath the skies today,
That the poorest of us here, when he goes to join the saints,

Will receive a touch of glory in the very self same way;
That the humblest of the lot
In the end won't be forgot,
As September crowns with beauty all the works of Mother Earth,
So the gentle God above,
In His mercy and His love,
In the frailest of his creatures will find something that's of worth.

¶ The man who keeps his troubles to himself at least robs his friends of something to gossip about.

BUSINESS

"BUSINESS is business," he said to me,
As he gave me short weight in my pound of tea.

"In business there is n't much sentiment,"
Said he, as he charged me the extra cent.

"Once I trusted a friend and he did n't pay,"
The bread that he sold was n't made that day.

"Business is business," he said to me,
Of a dozen eggs we could use but three.

O, it seems to me some way, somehow,
There 's too much business in business now.

THE SUMMER GIRL

THE Summer girl
In peek-a-boos
And open hose
And narrow shoes,
Now trips along
The sandy beach,
While each man mutters:
"She 's a peach."

And now she meets
A handsome man,
Who kindly stoops
To get her fan;
Thus is the romance
Quickly staged,
Next day, of course,
They are engaged.

In two short weeks
They separate,
Back to the daily
Grind they hate;
He to his office,
She the store,
And thus their brief
Engagement 's o'er.

He quite forgets
They ever met,
But she refuses
To forget;
She tells her friends,
With many a sigh:
"I almost had
A wealthy guy."

THE HOMES OF JOY

I LIKE the homes where a Teddy Bear
Monopolizes the best arm chair,
Where the sofa a rag doll occupies
And a train of cars in the corner lies;
For those are the signs that the home is glad
With a little girl or a little lad.

Give me the home that is all upset,
Where neatness is n't forever met,
Where a parlor floor is n't always straight
With its rugs in place. That 's as grim as Fate.
I want a home that is strewn with toys
Denoting the presence of girls and boys.

Let me gaze on buggies and Teddy Bears,
And dolls asleep in the company chairs;
Let me see in the corner, when I come in,
A battle front of soldiers tin
And a train of cars in a twisted heap,
And I 'll know that the youngsters are sound
asleep.

And I 'll be glad that you 've let me come
To the home of trumpet and horn and drum,
To the happy haunts where the children play,
I 'll be glad of the toys that are in my way;
My house is childless and neat, and yet
My heart with its toys still remains upset.

¶ Some men make the mistake of thinking they can never make one.

A SUCCESSFUL DAD

OTHERS may laugh at my feeble endeavor
To capture life's prizes, and others may sneer;
The whole world may loudly declare I shall never
Be worthy the gunpowder to blow me from here.
It may be I 'm punk as a parlor reciter,
And when I begin grown-ups take to the woods;
But that baby of mine! I can always delight her,
She vows I 'm a wonder, she swears I 'm the goods.

It may be I can't keep a tune for a minute,
It may be my voice wanders far from the key;
It may be the nightingale, lark and the linnet
As songsters have quite a wide margin on me.
Caruso and others may take down the money
For singing their ditties to high-brows, but I
Have one little audience, cheerful and sunny,
Who 'd rather hear me than the music you buy.

She thinks I 'm a corker, a lalapaloosa,
She nightly applauds every stunt that I do;
She 'd rather hear me than your John Philip Sousa,
To her the old nonsense forever is new.
That baby of mine thinks I 'm great in whatever
I tackle, the moment we 've finished our tea;
And though others may laugh at my feeble endeavor,
The praise of my little one satisfies me.

And so though the big world goes by me unheeding,
And never a grown-up takes notice of me;
Though into my work failure others are reading,
I 'm still a success to the babe on my knee.
When worn out and weary, my long day is ended,
And homeward I turn, I forget my distress;
For I know that my baby still thinks I am splendid,
To her, anyhow, I 'm a corking success!

DON'T YOU KNOW

H'IT'S h'easy to be 'appy,
Don't you know;
There's no sense in being snappy,
Don't you know;
Wot's the use h'of being grumpy,
H'or a bally rotter mumpy?
Folks don't like a fellow dumpy,
Don't you know.

H'every one h'as fits h'of sadness,
Don't you know;
No one's life h'is wholly gladness,
Don't you know;
H'if todye you taste h'of sorrow,
H'or a shilling 'ave to borrow,
Frowning won't 'elp things tomorrow,
Don't you know.

O, a gloomy cus h'is silly,
Don't you know;
'E's a downright balmy Billy,
Don't you know;
H'instead of h'alwyes moping
With 'is lips h'in downward sloping,
'E should smile h'and keep on 'oping,
Don't you know.

O, my word! H'if I were willing,
Don't you know,
H'every time h'I'd lack a shilling,
Don't you know,
H'in me wye so very 'umble,
H'I could start a dismal mumble,
But h'I larf --- h'I never grumble ---
Don't you know.

Tyke the time the guv'nor sacked me,
Don't you know;
Good h'old chap! 'E 'd alwyes backed me,
Don't you know;
'E got 'ot and sent me flying,
Cut me h'off --- there 's no use lying ---
But h'I larffed h'instead of crying,
Don't you know.

H'and h'I 'm 'ere on h'earth, still grinning,
Don't you know;
Back once more h'at the beginning,
Don't you know;
Tyking life the wye h'I find it,
Never arskin' wot 's be'ind it,
Though h'it 's 'ard h'I do not mind it,
Don't you know.

www.ingramcontent.com/pod-product-compliance
Lightning Source LLC
LaVergne TN
LVHW011225110826
845150LV00006B/1552